The Buddha's Path to Deliverance

Nyanatiloka Thera

About the Compiler

Ven. Nyanatiloka Thera was born in Germany in 1878 and was trained as a classical violinist in conservatories in Frankfort and Paris. After reading his first books on Buddhism, he immediately set his heart on becoming a Buddhist monk, and in 1903 he travelled to the East, where he took ordination in Burma. He thus became the first Continental European to join the Theravada Buddhist order. Ven. Nyanatiloka spent most of his monk's life in Sri Lanka, where in 1911 he established a monastery for Western Buddhist monks called Island Hermitage. He was a prolific translator of Pāli Buddhist texts into German and English. His other works published by the BPS include *Buddhist Dictionary*, *The Word of the Buddha*, *Guide through the Abhidhamma Pitaka*, and *Fundamentals of Buddhism*. He passed away in Colombo in 1957, after living for over fifty years as a distinguished member of the Theravada Buddhist order.

The Buddha's Path to Deliverance

A systematic exposition
in the words of the Sutta Piṭaka,
compiled, translated, and explained by

Nyanatiloka Thera

BPE

BPS Pariyatti Editions

BPS Pariyatti Editions
an imprint of
Pariyatti Publishing
www.pariyatti.org

First published by Buddhist Publication Society.
First Edition: 1952; Second revised edition: 1959;
Third edition: 1969; Fourth edition: 1982; Fifth edition: 2000

First BPS Pariyatti Edition, 2002
Third printing, 2009

ISBN: 978-1-681723-43-3 (softcover)

ISBN: 978-1-928706-32-8 (PDF eBook)

ISBN: 978-1-681720-50-0 (ePub eBook)

ISBN: 978-1-938754-63-0 (Mobi eBook)

Published under a copublishing agreement with the the original publisher, Buddhist Publication Society, Kandy, Sri Lanka.

Library of Congress Cataloging-in-Publication Data

Suttapiṭaka. English. Selections.
The Buddha's path to deliverance : a systematic exposition in the words of the Sutta piṭaka / Compiled, translated and explained by Nyanatiloka Thera
p. cm.
Originally published: Kandy: Buddhist Publication Society, 1952
Includes index
ISBN 978-1-928706-18-2 (alk. paper)
I.Title.

BQ1192.E53 B83 2001
294.3'823-DC21 2001035687

Contents

PREFACE IX

ABBREVIATIONS XII

THE BUDDHA'S MESSAGE 3

The Four Noble Truths 5

Appertaining to the First Truth 10

Appertaining to the third truth 23

Appertaining to the fourth truth 33

Threefold division of the path 41

1 MORALITY (*sīla*) 49

General Remarks 51

The Five Moral Precepts 52

Meat-Eating 53

The Eight Precepts 53

The Blessing of Morality 55

The Monk of Moral Perfection 56

I. Purity of Morality (*sīla-visuddhi*) 57

The Ascetical Means of Purification 58

2 CONCENTRATION (*samādhi*) 61

II. Purity of mind (*citta-visuddhi*) 63

General Remarks 63

Forty Concentration Exercises 64

Ten Kasiṇas 66

Eight Stages of Mastery (*abhibhāyatana*) 69

Perception of Light (*āloka-saññā*) 70

Ten cemetery meditations (Meditation on Loathsomeness) (*asubha-bhāvanā*) 70

The Ten Contemplations (*anussati*) 71

(1) Contemplation of the Buddha 73

(2) Contemplation of the Doctrine 73

(3) Contemplation of the Community 74

(4) Contemplation of Morality 74

(5) Contemplation of Liberality 74

(6) Contemplation of Heavenly Beings 74
(7) Contemplation of Death 75
(8) Contemplation of the Body 81
(9) Mindfulness of In-and-Out Breathing 83
(10) Contemplation of Peace 91
The Four Divine Abodes (*brahma-vihāra*) 93
I. Development of All-Embracing Kindness (*mettā-bhāvanā*) 93
The Hymn of Love 99
2. Development of Compassion 101
3. Development of Altruistic Joy 101
4. Development of Equanimity 102
Supplementary Texts 102
The Ten Perfections 105
Four Immaterial Spheres 107
Perception of Loathsomeness of food 111
The Early Teachers 113
Analysis of the four elements 114
The Four Applications of Mindfulness 115
The Eight Deliverances 120
Ten Contemplations 121
Overcoming and Developing 124
The Six Spiritual Powers 124
3 WISDOM (*paññā*) 127
General Remarks 129
Three Kinds of Wisdom 129
The Five Groups of Existence (*pañca khandha*) 130
Dependent Origination of the Five Groups 134
Inseparability of the Mental Groups 134
The Twelve Bases 135
The Eighteen Elements 137
The Twenty-Two Faculties 138
The Six Sense Faculties 139
Three Faculties 139
The Five Feeling Faculties 140
The Five Spiritual Faculties 141
Three Supramundane Faculties 143

The Four Noble Truths 143
Comprehension and Penetration 144
The First Truth 145
The Second and Third Truths 146
The Fourth Truth 147
The Dawn of Understanding 149
Dependent Origination 149
III. Purity of understanding 155
The Three Characteristics of Existence 156
Non-Self 157
Emptiness 158
Perfection of the Path 158
IV. Purity of Escape from doubt 160
Karma and Rebirth 162
V. Purity of knowledge and vision regarding path and not-path 165
VI. Purity of the knowledge and vision of progress 168
(2) contemplation of dissolution 169
(3) Awareness of terror 170
(4) Contemplation of misery 170
(5) Contemplation of turning away 171
(6) Desire for deliverance 172
(7) Reflective contemplation 172
(8) Equanimity regarding all formations 173
(9) Adaptation knowledge 178
The Thirty-Seven States Leading to Enlightenment 178
VII. Purity of knowledge and vision 179
The Ten Fetters and the Four Paths 180
The Simultaneous Understanding of the Truths . 182
The Early Masters (cited at Vism XXII,92) 182
Supplement 183
Cessation of Consciousness 183

INDEX 187

Preface

This book presents a systematically arranged outline of the entire teaching of the Buddha, given in the words found in the earliest records, the Sutta Piṭaka (Discourse Collection) of the Pāli Canon. A shorter, likewise systematically arranged anthology was published by the author in the German language, already in 1906, under the title *Das Wort des Buddha* (*The Word of the Buddha*). Since then it has been translated into many languages such as English, French, Italian, Czech, Finnish, Japanese, Hindi, and Bengali; an edition of the original Pāli texts collected in that book was published in Sinhala and Devanagari script.

While *The Word of the Buddha* presents the doctrine in the framework of the Four Noble Truths, in the present book, after a summary of the Four Truths, the arrangement is according to a threefold division of the Noble Eightfold Path, i.e. morality, concentration, and wisdom, *sīla, samādhi, paññā.* In that sequence, these three divisions are the natural stages of progress in the perfecting of the Noble Eightfold Path.

At the same time, there runs through the whole book, like a red thread, the teaching of the seven stages of purity (*satta visuddhi*) by which the threefold training in higher morality, mentality, and wisdom is brought to highest perfection. These seven stages of purity are also the framework of the great commentator Buddhaghosa's (5th century A.C.) monumental work, *Visuddhimagga*, "The Path of Purification," and for additional details, particularly on the last five stages of purity, reference to that great compendium of the entire doctrine is recommended.

The texts translated in this present anthology have been drawn from all five collections (nikāya) of the Sutta Piṭaka. Regarding the fifth collection, the author has gathered a number of texts from the Khuddakapāṭha, Dhammapada, Sutta-nipāta, Udāna, Itivuttaka, Paṭisambhidāmagga, and also from the Milindapañha. Of all the books, the Aṅguttara Nikāya proved the richest mine of information. A considerable number of very important texts has also been taken from the Saṃyutta Nikāya. As it was difficult at times to find suitable old sutta texts for the higher stages of purity, the author was compelled to use a few texts from the Paṭisambhidāmagga which, though listed amongst the books of the Khuddaka Nikāya, is undoubtedly apocryphal. However, only such texts have been quoted from it as have the genuine character of the suttas.

The extracts and references contained in the explanatory notes have been taken mostly from the author's works and translations, mainly from his German translation of the Visuddhimagga, partly from the Paṭisambhidāmagga, Vibhaṅga, and other works, but here and there also from the "Early Masters" cited in the Visuddhimagga.

For reasons of arrangement it was sometimes not possible to avoid a repeated treatment of some subjects, such as karma, *paṭicca-samuppāda*, the Four Noble Truths, etc. But in conformity with the gradual development of the path, these doctrines are at first given in mere outline, and, more or less, in conventional language (*vohāra*); but in later chapters in connection with the higher stages of knowledge, they are explained in strict philosophical language (*paramattha*) as used in the Abhidhamma, the third of the three "Baskets" of the Pāli Canon.

Though the Abhidhamma Piṭaka doubtlessly represents a later development of the original teachings, it nevertheless contradicts in no essential point the teachings laid down in the Sutta Piṭaka, but on the contrary helps towards a correct understanding of the older texts. Particularly those passages in the present book which deal with the higher stages of knowledge will clearly show that a considerable part of Abhidhamma doctrine is already contained, at least in seed form, in the Sutta Piṭaka. This will help to bring out strongly the impressive inner consistency of the whole edifice of Buddhist doctrine.

For one who masters the Pāli language and has thoroughly studied and digested the voluminous body of the canonical texts, both of Sutta and Abhidhamma, and is also familiar with the Visuddhimagga and other commentaries, there can no longer exist any doubt or uncertainty regarding the essential teachings of the Buddha. For the same reason, no difference of opinion about the Buddha's doctrine can exist among the Buddhist scholars of Southern Asia. That, on the other hand, many Western authors and critics, in their interpretations of Buddhist doctrine, so often contradict each other, is due to the fact that they lack the aforementioned primary conditions. This applies, in particular, to the understanding of those central Buddhist doctrines of non-self (*anattā*) and dependent origination (*paṭicca-samuppāda*). It is hoped that the texts presented here will contribute to a correct grasp of these two important doctrines and, in general, will be a help in the study and a stimulus towards the practice of the liberating teachings of the Enlightened One.

NYANATILOKA
Island Hermitage
Dodanduva, Lanka (Ceylon)
January 1950

Abbreviations

AN	Aṅguttara Nikāya (figures refer to nipāta and sutta)
DN	Dīgha Nikāya (number of sutta)
Dhp	Dhammapada (number of verse)
It	Itivuttaka (number of sutta)
Mil	Milindapañha
MN	Majjhima Nikāya (number of sutta)
Pṭs	Paṭisambhidāmagga (niddeso and paragraph)
Pug	Puggalapaññatti
SN	Saṃyutta Nikāya (number of saṃyutta and sutta)
Snp	Suttanipāta (number of verse)
Ud	Udāna (vagga and number of sutta)
Vibh	Vibhaṅga (vibhaṅga and paragraph)
Vism	Visuddhimagga (chapter and paragraph)
B. Dict.	*Buddhist Dictionary* (Nyanatiloka)
Fund.	*Fundamentals of Buddhism* (Nyanatiloka)
Guide	*Guide through the Abhidhamma Piṭaka* (Nyanatiloka)

The Buddha's Path to Deliverance

The Buddha's Message

THE BUDDHA'S MESSAGE:
THE FOUR NOBLE TRUTHS
(*cattāri ariya-saccāni*)

§1 All the doctrines of the Buddha are handed down to us in the three collections of books written in the Pāli language, the so-called Tipiṭaka, lit. the "Three Baskets." These are: (1) the Vinaya Piṭaka, or books on monastic discipline; (2) the Sutta Piṭaka, or books of discourses; (3) the Abhidhamma Piṭaka, or books on ultimate truths. Apart from the books and sections dealing with the rules and regulations of monks' life, the Buddhist scriptures contain, correctly speaking, nothing but expositions and explanations of the Four Noble Truths and the path to deliverance, constituting the true and genuine teaching of the Buddha. On these therefore the present book has been built up. The Four Noble Truths are:

I. The truth about suffering
II. The truth about the origin of suffering
III. The truth about the cessation of suffering
IV. The truth about the path leading to the cessation of suffering, i.e.:

<table>
<tr><td>1. Right understanding (sammā-diṭṭhi)</td><td rowspan="2">} Wisdom (paññā)</td></tr>
<tr><td>2. Right thought (sammā-saṅkappa)</td></tr>
<tr><td>3. Right speech (sammā-vācā)</td><td rowspan="3">} Morality (sīla)</td></tr>
<tr><td>4. Right bodily action (sammā-kammanta)</td></tr>
<tr><td>5. Right livelihood (sammā-ājīva)</td></tr>
<tr><td>6. Right effort (sammā-vāyāma)</td><td rowspan="3">} Concentration (samādhi)</td></tr>
<tr><td>7. Right mindfulness (sammā-sati)</td></tr>
<tr><td>8. Right concentration (sammā-samādhi)</td></tr>
</table>

The first truth, briefly stated, teaches that the whole of existence, which is comprised without remainder in the so-called five groups of existence (*pañcakhandha,* i.e. corporeality, feeling, perception, mental formations, and consciousness), is something miserable and subject to suffering, impermanent, impersonal, and void.

The second truth teaches that all suffering, in other words, the whole of existence, is conditioned through craving (*taṇhā*), which produces rebirth and suffering, and which is manifested as volitional activities, or karma, of body, speech, or mind. The second truth, therefore, comprises also the doctrine of karma and rebirth, as well as the law of dependent origination (*paṭicca-samuppāda*) of all the phenomena of existence.

The third truth teaches that the utter cessation of this selfish craving for life, and of all forms of delusion connected with it, must necessarily lead to deliverance from rebirth and suffering, i.e. to the realization of Nibbāna.

The fourth truth about the above-mentioned Noble Eightfold Path shows the path, or means, to deliverance from suffering. It contains the entire Buddhist practice.

§2 Not Understanding Four Things

(DN 16)

It is through not understanding, not penetrating four things, O monks, that I as well as you had to wander so long through this round of rebirths. And what are these four things?

They are: the noble truth of suffering, the noble truth of the origin of suffering, the noble truth of the cessation of suffering, and the noble truth of the (eightfold) path leading to the cessation of suffering.

Through not understanding, not penetrating these Four Noble Truths, O monks, I as well as you had to wander so long through this round of rebirths.

About the round of rebirths see B. Dict. *saṃsāra.*

§3 The Four Truths

(DN 22; MN 141)

(I) What now, O monks, is the noble truth of suffering? Birth is suffering, old age is suffering, death is suffering, sorrow, lamentation, pain, grief, and despair are suffering. Not to get what one desires is suffering, in short: the five groups of existence forming the objects of attachment (*pañc'upādāna-*

khandha) are suffering, namely, the corporeality group, the feeling group, the perception group, the mental formations group, the consciousness group.

§4 (II) But what, O monks, is the noble truth of the origin of suffering? It is that craving which gives rise to fresh rebirth and, bound up with pleasure and lust, now here, now there, finds ever fresh delight. It is sensual craving, craving for existence, and craving for self-annihilation.

Craving for existence" (*bhava-taṇhā*) is craving connected with the eternity view (*sassata-diṭṭhi*)—i.e. the spiritualistic belief in an eternal self or soul that still continues after death.

"Craving for self-annihilation" (*vibhava-taṇhā*) is craving connected with the self-annihilation view (*uccheda-vāda* or *vibhava-diṭṭhi*)—i.e. the materialistic belief in a temporary self that will become annihilated at death.

The Buddha, however, neither teaches an eternal self, nor a temporary self, but he teaches that our existence consists in a mere process of mental and physical phenomena, and that there is nowhere to be found any real and independent ego-entity.

§5 (III) But what, O monks, is the noble truth of the cessation of suffering? It is the complete fading away and cessation of this craving, its forsaking and giving up, liberation and detachment from it.

For, through the total fading away and cessation of craving, clinging is extinguished; through the cessation of clinging, the process of becoming is extinguished; through the cessation of the (karmic) process of becoming, rebirth is extinguished; through the cessation of rebirth, decay and death, sorrow, lamentation, pain, grief, and despair are extinguished. Thus comes about the cessation of this whole mass of suffering (SN 12:1).

§6 (IV) But what, O monks, is the noble truth of the path leading to the cessation of suffering? It is the Noble Eightfold Path, namely: right understanding, right thought, right speech, right bodily action, right livelihood, right effort, right mindfulness, and right concentration.

§7 (1) But what, O monks, is right understanding (*sammā-diṭṭhi*)? To understand suffering, to understand the origination of suffering, to understand the cessation of suffering, to understand the path leading to the cessation of suffering: this is called right understanding.

§8 (2) But what, O monks, is right thought (*sammā-saṅkappa*)? Thoughts free from sensuous desire, thoughts free from ill-will, thoughts free from cruelty: this is called right thought.

§9 (3) But what, O monks, is right speech (*sammā-vācā*)? Abstaining from lying, from tale-bearing, from harsh language, and from vain talk: this is called right speech.

AN 4:149 gives these four kinds of speech in positive language: truthful speech, conciliatory speech, mild speech, and wise speech.

§10 (4) But what, O monks, is right bodily action (*sammā-kammanta*)? Abstaining from destroying life, from stealing, and from sexual misconduct: this is called right bodily action.

§11 (5) But what, O monks, is right livelihood (*sammā- ājīva*)? When the noble disciple, avoiding a wrong way of living, gets his livelihood by a right way of living: this is called right livelihood.

"Five kinds of trade should be avoided by the disciple: trading in arms, in living beings, in meat, in intoxicating drinks, and in poisons" (AN 5:177).

"What is wrong livelihood? Gaining one's livelihood by deceiving, persuasive words, hints, slandering, eagerly hankering after ever greater gain: this is wrong livelihood" (MN 117).

These latter five practices are fully explained in Vism I, 61–65 and illustrated with regard to the monk's wrong livelihood. Cf. §70.

§12 (6) But what, O monks, is right effort (*sammā-vāyāma*)? Herein, the monk rouses his mind to avoid evil, unwholesome things not yet arisen—to overcome evil, unwholesome things already arisen—to arouse wholesome things not yet arisen—to maintain wholesome things already arisen and not to let them disappear, but to bring them to growth, to maturity, and to the full perfection of development. And he makes effort, puts forth his energy, exerts his mind, and strives. This is called right effort.

The first effort consists in avoiding greed, etc., by means of sense restraint; the second in overcoming greed, etc.; the third in developing the seven factors of enlightenment (s. §202); the fourth in maintaining all wholesome states.

§13 (7) But what, O monks, is right mindfulness (*sammā-sati*)? Herein the monk dwells in contemplation of the body—the feelings—the mind—mind-objects, ardent, clearly conscious and mindful, after putting away worldly greed and grief.

§14 (8) But what, O monks, is right concentration (*sammā-samādhi*)? Herein the monk, detached from sensual objects, detached from unwholesome things, enters into the first absorption (*jhāna*), born of detachment, accompanied by thought-conception (*vitakka*) and discursive thinking (*vicāra*), and filled with rapture (*pīti*) and joy (*sukha*).

After the subsiding of thought-conception and discursive thinking, and by gaining inner tranquillity and oneness of the mind, he enters into a state free from thought-conception and discursive thinking, the second absorption, which is born of concentration (*samādhi*) and filled with rapture and joy.

After the fading away of rapture, he dwells in equanimity, mindful, clearly conscious; and he experiences in his person that feeling of which the noble ones say, "Happy is the man of equanimity who is mindful"—thus he enters the third absorption.

After the giving up of pleasure and pain, and through the disappearance of previous joy and grief, he enters into a state beyond pleasure and pain, into the fourth absorption, which is purified by equanimity (*upekkhā*) and mindfulness. This is right concentration.

> If here only the four absorptions (*jhāna*) are called right concentration, it is done so in the sense of a prominent example. In its widest sense, however, one has to understand by right concentration that concentration which is associated with all karmically wholesome consciousness whatever. The different stages in the development of right concentration and the four *jhānas* will be treated later.

This is called the truth about the path leading to the cessation of suffering.

APPERTAINING TO THE FIRST TRUTH

§15 **The Three Heavenly Messengers**

AN 3:35

Did you never see in the world a man or a woman, eighty, ninety, or a hundred years old, frail, crooked as a gable roof, bent down, resting on crutches, with tottering steps, infirm, youth long since fled, with broken teeth, grey and scanty hair or none, wrinkled, with blotched limbs? And did the thought never come to you that you too are subject to decay, that you too cannot escape it?

Did you never see in the world a man or a woman, sick, afflicted, grievously ill, wallowing in his own filth, lifted up by some, and put to bed by others? And did the thought never come to you that you too are subject to sickness, that you too cannot escape it?

Did you never see in the world the corpse of a man, one, two, or three days after death, swollen up, blue-black in colour, and full of corruptions? And did the thought never come to you that you too are subject to death, that you too cannot escape it?

The three heavenly messengers (*deva-dūta*)—old age, sickness, and death—are in Buddhist countries often allegorically represented in fresco and sculpture. In MN 130 we find, besides these three, two more, namely birth and the punishment of criminals.

§16 The Inflexible Law of Nature

AN 4:182

Four things, O monks, nobody can bring about, no ascetic, brahmin, or heavenly being, no god nor devil nor anyone in this world. And what are these four things?

That what is subject to decay may not decay—that what is subject to sickness may not fall sick—that what is subject to death may not die—that those evil, impure, frightful, and pain-bestowing actions, which ever and again lead to rebirth, old age, and death, may not bring results. These four things, O monks, nobody can bring about, no ascetic, brahmin, or heavenly being, no god nor devil nor anyone in this world.

§17 The Immensity of Saṃsāra

SN 15:3, 13, 10

Inconceivable is the beginning of this *saṃsāra*; not to be discovered is a first beginning of beings who, obstructed by ignorance and ensnared by craving, are hurrying and hastening through this round of rebirths.

§18 Which do you think, O monks, is more: the flood of tears which, weeping and wailing, you have shed upon this long way—hurrying and hastening through this round of rebirths, united with the undesired, separated from the desired—this, or the waters of the four great oceans?

Long have you suffered the death of father and mother, of sons, daughters, brothers, and sisters. And while you were thus suffering you have, indeed, shed more tears upon this long way than there is water in the four great oceans.

§19 Which do you think is more: the streams of blood that, through your being beheaded, have flowed upon this long way—this, or the waters in the four great oceans?

Long have you been caught as robbers, or highwaymen, or adulterers; and through your being beheaded, truly more blood has flowed upon this long way than there is water in the four great oceans.

And thus, O monks, have you long undergone suffering, undergone torment, undergone misfortune, and filled the graveyards full; truly, long enough to be dissatisfied with all forms of existence, long enough to turn away and free yourselves from them all.

§20 If one were to heap up all the bones of one single living being during its hurrying and hastening for one single world-period through this round of rebirths, and the bones were not to decay, there would arise a mountain of bones as big as this Vepulla mountain.

And how is this possible? Inconceivable is the beginning of this *saṃsāra*; not to be discovered is a first beginning of beings who, obstructed by ignorance and ensnared by craving, are hurrying and hastening through this round of rebirths.

§21 Duration of One World-Period

SN 15:5

Long, O monks, lasts one world-period (*kappa*, Skt *kalpa*), and it is not possible to count it as so many years, so many centuries, so many millenia, so many hundred millenia. Suppose there was a mighty rock, one mile deep, one mile wide, one mile high, without breaches or crevices, of one solid mass. And whenever a hundred years have elapsed, a man would come and rub against this rock only once with a little silken cloth. Then this mighty rock would vanish quicker than one world-period lasts. This is the duration of one world-period. But through many such world-periods, O monks, have you hurried and hastened, through many hundreds, many thousands, many hundred thousands. And how is this possible?

Inconceivable, O monks, is the beginning of this *saṃsāra;* not to be discovered is a first beginning of beings who, obstructed by ignorance and ensnared by craving, are hurrying and hastening through this round of rebirths.

Here the reader may remember that beautiful allegory in Grimm's fairy tale of the little shepherd boy: "In farther Pommerania there is a diamond mountain, one hour high, one hour wide, one hour deep. There every hundred years a little bird comes and whets its little beak on it. And when the whole mountain is ground off, then the first second of eternity has passed."

§22 Kinship with All

SN 15:14–19

Not easy is it, O monks, to find any living being that upon this long round of rebirths has not yet, sometime or other, been your mother, or father, or brother, or sister, or son, or daughter. And how is this possible? Inconceivable, O monks, is the beginning of this *saṃsāra;* not to be discovered is a first beginning of beings who, obstructed by ignorance and ensnared by craving, are hurrying and hastening through this round of rebirths.

§23 The Three Characteristics of Existence

SN 18:1

What do you think, Rāhula: are eye, ear, nose, tongue, body, and mind permanent or impermanent?

"Impermanent, O Venerable One."

Are corporeality, feeling, perception, mental formations, and consciousness permanent or impermanent?

"Impermanent, O Venerable One."

But what is impermanent, is this happiness or suffering?

"Suffering, O Venerable One."

But of that which is impermanent, suffering, and subject to change, can one rightly hold the view: "This belongs to me, this am I, this is my self"?

"No, O Venerable One."

Understanding thus, Rāhula, the noble disciple turns away from these things; and through his turning away therefrom, he becomes detached; and through his being detached, he is liberated; and through his being liberated, the knowledge arises in him: "Liberated am I." And he knows: "Rebirth has ceased, the holy life is fulfilled, the task is done, and nothing further remains after this."

§24 Unreality of the Self

SN 22:15

Corporeality, feeling, perception, mental formations, and consciousness are impermanent. And whatever is impermanent is suffering. And whatever is suffering is non-self. And of that which is non-self, one should understand according to reality, and with true wisdom: "This does not belong to me, this am I not, this is not my self."

§25 Cessation

SN 22:21

Corporeality, feeling, perception, mental formations, and consciousness are impermanent, produced, have a dependent origination, are subject to perishing, destruction, disappearance, and cessation.

And because these things come to cessation, therefore one speaks of "cessation."

§26 Discourse on Non-Self

(*Anattālakkhaṇa Sutta*)

SN 22:59

Once the Blessed One dwelt at the Seers' Ascent (Isipatana), in the Deer Park near Benares. There the Blessed One spoke thus to the five monks (with whom he formerly had practised bodily mortification):

Corporeality is non-self. If corporeality were a self, then corporeality would not lead to affliction, and one would succeed in one's wish: "Thus my corporeality shall be, thus shall it not be!" But as corporeality is non-self, therefore corporeality leads to affliction, and one cannot succeed in one's wish: "Thus my corporeality shall be, thus shall it not be!"

Feeling is non-self ... Perception is non-self ... Mental formations are non-self ...

Consciousness is non-self. If consciousness were a self, then consciousness would not lead to affliction, and one would succeed in one's wish: "Thus my consciousness shall be, thus shall it not be!" But as consciousness is non-self, therefore consciousness leads to affliction, and one cannot succeed in one's wish: "Thus my consciousness shall be, thus shall it not be!"

Understanding thus, the noble disciple turns away from these things; and through his turning away, he becomes detached; and through his being detached, he is liberated; and through his being liberated, the knowledge arises in him: "Liberated am I." And he knows: "Rebirth has ceased, the holy life is fulfilled, the task is done, and nothing further remains after this."

§27 Appertaining to the second truth

Dependent Origination of Suffering

MN 38

Through what is this craving (*taṇhā*) brought about, through what condition does it arise, spring up, and enter into existence? Through feeling.

And feeling (*vedanā*)? Through (sensorial or mental) impression.

And impression (*phassa*)? Through the six bases.

And the six bases (*āyatana*)? Through mind and corporeality.

And mind and corporeality (*nāma-rūpa*)? Through consciousness.

And consciousness (*viññāṇa*; beginning from the moment of conception)? Through the karma-formations.

And the karma-formations (*saṅkhāra*)? Through ignorance (*avijjā*).

Thus, conditioned by ignorance are the karma-formations; by the karma-formations, consciousness; by consciousness, mind and corporeality; by mind and corporeality, the six bases; by the six bases, (sensorial and mental) impression; by impression, feeling; by feeling, craving; by craving, clinging; by clinging, (the karma-process and rebirth-process of) becoming; by (the karma-process of) becoming, rebirth; by rebirth, old age and death, sorrow, lamentation, pain, grief, and despair. Thus arises this whole mass of suffering.

In AN 3:61, the second noble truth is given by way of this formula of dependent origination thus: "But what, O monks, is the noble truth of the origin of suffering? Conditioned by ignorance are the karma-formations; by the karma-formations, consciousness, etc. For a detailed exposition of dependent origination, see §168 ff.

§28 Craving, the Cause of Suffering

MN 13

Truly, due to sensuous craving, conditioned by sensuous craving, impelled by sensuous craving, entirely moved by sensuous craving, kings fight with kings, princes with princes, brahmins with brahmins, citizens with citizens; mother quarrels with son, son with mother; father with son, son with father; brother with brother, brother with sister, sister with brother, friend with friend. Thus, given to dissension, quarreling, and fighting, they fall upon one another with fists, sticks, or weapons. And thereby they suffer death or deadly pain.

And further, due to sensuous craving, people break into houses, rob, plunder, pillage whole houses, commit highway robbery, seduce the wives of others. Then the rulers have such people caught and inflict on them various forms of punishment. And thereby they incur death or deadly pain. Now this is the misery of sensuous craving, the heaping up of suffering in this present life, due to sensuous craving.

And further, people take to the evil way in deeds, words, and thoughts; and thus, at the dissolution of the body after death, they fall into a downward state of existence, a state of suffering, into perdition, and the abyss of hell. But this is the misery of sensuous craving, the heaping up of suffering in the future life, due to sensuous craving.

§29 Karma and Rebirth

AN 10:205

Beings are owners of their deeds (*kamma*, Skt *karma*), heirs of their deeds, their deeds are the womb from which they sprang, they are bound up with their deeds, their deeds are their refuge. Whatever deeds they do—good or evil—of such they will be the heirs.

There is one who destroys living beings, takes what belongs to others, has unlawful intercourse with the other sex; speaks untruth, is a tale-bearer, uses harsh language, is an empty prattler; is covetous, cruel-minded, follows evil views.

And he is creeping in his actions by body, speech, and mind. Hidden are his deeds, words, and thoughts, hidden his ways and objects. But I tell you: whoever pursues hidden ways and objects will have to expect one of these two results: either the torments of hell, or birth among the creeping animals.

Thus it is with the rebirth of beings: they will be reborn according to their deeds (*kamma*). And having been reborn, they will experience the result of their deeds. Therefore I declare: beings are owners and heirs of their deeds, their deeds are the womb from which they sprang, they are bound up with their deeds, their deeds are their refuge. Whatever deeds they do—good or evil—of such they will be the heirs.

§30 Rebirth According to Karma

MN 135

Beings are owners and heirs of their deeds ... deeds divide beings into the lofty and the low.

There is one—woman or man—who destroys living beings, is cruel, addicted to beating and killing, without love for living beings. Through such deeds, however carried out or undertaken, this being, at the dissolution of the body after death, will fall into a low state of existence, a woeful course of life, into perdition, or hell ... or, if reborn as a human being, he will, wherever he enters into existence, be of short life.

There is one who has the habit of causing pain to other beings by means of fist, stone, stick, or sword. Through such deeds he will fall into a low state of existence ... or, if reborn as a human being, he will, wherever he enters into existence, have much sickness.

There is one who is hot-tempered, flies quickly into a passion; at the slightest thing told to him he gets into a rage, is angry, stubborn, shows excitement, hatred, and suspicion. Through such deeds he will fall into a low state of existence ... or, if reborn as a human being he will, wherever he enters into existence, have an ugly appearance.

There is one who is envious, full of jealousy and animosity, who feels envy at that which others receive as gifts, hospitality, honour, veneration, respectful salutation, and gracious offerings. Through such deeds he will fall into a low state of existence ... or, if reborn as a human being, he will, wherever he enters into existence, possess only little influence.

There is one who offers to monks and brahmins no food, drink, robes, conveyances, flowers, perfumes, ointment, bed, dwelling, lamps, and accessories. Through such deeds he will fall into a low state of existence ... Or, if reborn as a human being, he will, wherever he enters into existence, be without wealth.

There is one who is haughty and full of vanity, does not salute whom he should salute, nor rise before whom he should rise, nor offer a seat to whom a seat should be offered, nor make room for whom he should make room, nor feast whom he ought to feast, nor respect and honour those to whom honour and respect are due, nor make gifts to those to whom gifts should be made. Through such deeds he will fall into a low state of existence ... or, if reborn as a human being, he will, wherever he enters into existence, be of low birth.

There is one who does not visit monks and brahmins and put them questions: "What, O Venerable One, is karmically wholesome? What unwholesome? What blameworthy?

What blameless? What should one practise? What not? Which practice will lead me for a long time to harm and suffering? Which to blessing and happiness?" Through such deeds he will fall into a low state of existence ... or if reborn as a human being, he will, wherever he enters into existence, be without intelligence.

§31 Differences Among Women

AN 4:197

"What, O Venerable One, is the cause and reason that a woman is ugly, of ugly appearance, most evil to look at; and is poor, without power, wealth, and influence? And what is the cause and reason that a woman is ugly...; but is rich, with great power, wealth, and influence? And what is the cause and reason that a woman is beautiful, fair to behold, of grace and exceeding beauty of complexion; but is poor, without power, wealth, and influence? And what is the cause and reason that a woman is beautiful...; and is rich, with great power, wealth, and influence?"

There is, Mallikā, a woman who is hot-tempered, who flies quickly into a rage; at the slightest thing told to her, she gets into a rage, is angry, stubborn, shows excitement, hatred, and suspicion. And she does not provide monks and brahmins with food and drink, with robes, conveyances, flowers, perfume, ointment, bed, dwelling, lamps, and accessories; she is full of envy, jealousy, and animosity, feels envy at that which others receive as gifts, hospitality, honour, veneration, respectful salutation, and gracious offerings. Should this woman, after death, return to this world, she will, wherever she is reborn, be ugly, of ugly appearance, most evil to look at, and she will be poor, without power, wealth, and influence.

There is another woman who is hot-tempered, who flies quickly into a rage ... But she provides monks and brahmins with food and drink ... and is without envy and jealousy.... Should this woman, after death, return to this world, she will, wherever she is reborn, be ugly...; but she will be rich, with great power, wealth, and influence.

There is another woman who is not hot-tempered, who does not fly quickly into a rage.... But she does not provide monks and brahmins with food and drink.... Should this woman, after death, return to this world, she will, wherever she is reborn, be beautiful, fair to behold, endowed with grace and exceeding beauty of complexion. But she will be poor, without power, wealth, and influence.

There is another woman who is not hot-tempered, who does not fly quickly into a rage.... And she provides monks and brahmins with food and drink ... and is without envy and jealousy.... Should this woman, after death, return to this world, she will, wherever she is reborn, be beautiful, fair to behold, endowed with grace and exceeding beauty of complexion. And she will be rich, with great power, wealth, and influence.

> According to MN 136, even a so-called evil-doer who has, immediately before the death-moment, a karmically wholesome thought, may be reborn for a short period of time in some higher world; and, conversely, a good person who has an evil thought just before death may be reborn in a lower world.

§32 Results of Immoral Actions

AN 8:40

The destroying of living beings, O monks, committed, carried out, and often pursued, leads to hell, the animal world, or the realm of ghosts. Even the least result of destroying living beings brings a short life.

The taking of other people's belongings, committed, carried out, and often pursued, leads to hell, the animal world, or the realm of ghosts. Even the least result of taking other people's belongings brings the loss of one's goods.

Unlawful sexual intercourse, committed, carried out, and often pursued, leads to hell, the animal world, or the realm of ghosts. Even the least result of unlawful sexual intercourse brings enmity with one's rivals.

Lying, committed, carried out, and often pursued, leads to hell, the animal world, or the realm of ghosts. Even the least result of lying brings false accusations.

Tale-bearing, committed, carried out, and often pursued, leads to hell, the animal world, or the realm of ghosts. Even the least result of tale-bearing brings discord with one's friends.

Harsh language, committed, carried out, and often pursued, leads to hell, the animal world, or the realm of ghosts. Even the least result of harsh language brings exposure to displeasing words.

Vain prattle, committed, carried out, and often pursued, leads to hell, the animal world, or the realm of ghosts. Even the least result of vain prattle brings one to hear unacceptable words.

Taking intoxicating drinks, such as wine and liquor, committed, carried out, and often pursued, leads to hell, the animal world, or the realm of ghosts. Even the least result of taking intoxicating drinks brings insanity.

§33 The Three Roots of Evil Action

AN 3:33

There are, O monks, three root-conditions for the doing of actions (*kamma*), namely: greed (*lobha*), hate (*dosa*), and delusion (*moha*).

> In AN 3:68 it is said that through unwise reflection on an attractive object, there may arise greed; and through unwise reflection on a repulsive object, there may arise hate. Thus, in its widest sense, the term *lobha* comprises all degrees of attraction, from the slightest trace of attachment up to the crassest forms of greed and egoism, while the term *dosa* comprises all degrees of aversion, from the slightest touch of ill-humour up to the extreme forms of violent wrath and revenge.

The action, O monks, that is done out of greed, that has arisen through greed, that is produced by greed, this action will ripen wherever the being is reborn; and wherever the action ripens, there the being reaps the fruit of that action, be it in this life, or in the next life, or in future lives.

The action that is done out of hate, that has arisen through hate, that is produced by hate, this action will ripen wherever the being is reborn; and wherever the action ripens, there the being reaps the fruit of that action, be it in this life, or in the next life, or in future lives.

The action that is done out of delusion, that has arisen through delusion, that is produced by delusion, this action will ripen wherever the being is reborn; and wherever the action ripens, there the being reaps the fruit of that action, be it in this life, or in the next life, or in future lives.

It is just as with unhurt and unspoiled seed, undamaged by wind and the sun's heat, healthy and well preserved, which, after being sown in rich soil and well-prepared ground, will, owing to plentiful rainfall, shoot up, attain growth and full development.

§34 Causes of Rebirth

SN 22:99

There will come a time, O monks, when this mighty ocean will dry up, disappear, and be no more. But there will be no end of suffering to beings who, obstructed by ignorance and fettered by craving, are hurrying and hastening thorough this round of rebirths. Thus I say.

There will come a time when this mighty earth will be devoured by fire, destroyed, and be no more. But there will be no end of suffering to beings who, obstructed by ignorance and fettered by craving, are hurrying and hastening through this round of rebirths. Thus I say.

§35 Cessation of Karma

AN 10:208

It is not possible, O monks, I say, that willed, performed, and heaped-up actions (*kamma*) come to cessation as long as one has not yet experienced their results, be it in this life, or in the next life, or in future lives. And it is not possible, I say, that without having oneself experienced the results of the willed, performed, and heaped-up actions, one can put an end to suffering.

APPERTAINING TO THE THIRD TRUTH

§36 Dependent Cessation of Suffering

AN 3:61

What, O monks, is the cessation of suffering? Through the complete overcoming and cessation of ignorance (*avijjā*) there comes about the cessation of karma-formations; through the cessation of karma-formations (*saṅkhārā*), the cessation of consciousness (after death); through the cessation of consciousness (*viññāṇa*), the cessation of mind and corporeality; through the cessation of mind and corporeality (*nāma-rūpa*), the cessation of the six bases (sense-organs and mind); through the cessation of the six bases (*saḷāyatana*), the cessation of (sensorial and mental) impression; through the cessation of impression (*phassa*), the cessation of feeling; through the cessation of feeling (*vedanā*), the cessation of craving; through the cessation of craving (*taṇhā*), the cessation of clinging; through the cessation of clinging (*upādāna*), the cessation of (the karma-process and rebirth-process of) becoming; through the cessation of (the karma-process of becoming (*bhava*), the cessation of rebirth; through the cessation of rebirth (*jāti*) comes about the cessation of old age and death (*jarā-maraṇa*), sorrow, lamentation, pain, grief, and despair. Thus comes about the cessation of this whole mass of suffering.

This, O monks, is called the noble truth of the cessation of suffering.

On dependent origination see §§168–74.

§37 Nibbāna

AN 3:32

There, Ānanda, the monk considers thus: "This is peace, this is the sublime, namely the standstill of all karma formations, the forsaking of all substrata of existence, the fading away of craving, detachment, cessation, Nibbāna."

Thus, Ānanda, the monk may attain such a concentration of mind wherein with regard to this body endowed with consciousness and with regard to all external objects, no impulses of "I" and "mine," and no attacks of conceit can come upon him, and wherein he is in possession of that deliverance of mind and that deliverance through wisdom wherein no impulses of "I" and "mine," and no more attacks of conceit can come upon him. The following, however, I have replied to the question about the goal:

> Who is not troubled any more
> And knows both good and bad,
> Stilled, freed from wrath, grief and desire,
> He has escaped old age and death.

(Snp 1048)

§38 The Visible Nibbāna

AN 3:55

Through greed, hate, and delusion, overwhelmed by greed, hate, and delusion, one aims at one's own ruin, at others' ruin, at the ruin of both, and one suffers mental pain and grief. If, however, greed, hate, and delusion are given up, one aims neither at one's own ruin, nor at others' ruin, nor at the ruin of both, and one suffers no more mental pain and grief.

Thus is Nibbāna realizable even during lifetime, immediate, inviting, attractive, and comprehensible to the wise. Now, in so far as the monk has realized the complete cessation of greed, hate, and delusion, in so far is Nibbāna realizable, immediate, inviting, attractive, and comprehensible to the wise.

§39 Unshakable

AN 6:55

Should, O Venerable One, to a monk thus liberated in mind, even extraordinarily sublime and mighty visible forms come into his field of vision, sounds into his field of hearing, odours into his field of smelling, flavours into his field of tasting, bodily impressions into his field of bodily touch, mentally cognizable objects into his field of mind, all these things can no longer overwhelm his mind. His mind remains untouched, steadfast, unshakable, beholding the impermanence of everything.

One who has turned to renunciation,
Turned to detachment of the mind,
Is filled with all-embracing love,
And freed from thirsting after life,

Has turned to quitting all desire,
To unobstructed sight of mind,
Knowing the senses' origin;
His mind, indeed, is fully freed.

And such a monk with mind thus freed,
Who found the stillness of his heart,
Heaps up no more the deeds he did,
And naught remains for him to do.

Just as a big and solid rock
Cannot be shaken by the wind,
So visual forms, sounds, or smells,
Tastes and bodily impressions,

Lovely things or ugly things,
Can no more shake the holy one.
Firm is his mind, his mind is freed,
He sees how all things pass away.

§40 The Elder

AN 4:22

Whoever possesses perfect virtue,
Is clever and endowed with wit,
Restrained and firm in all good things,
And wisely penetrates the truth,

Who fully understands all things,
The wise one from obstructions freed,
Delivered from rebirth and death,
Who has attained the holy goal:

Him do I call an Elder
Who has abandoned all taints,
In whom all the taints have ceased:
That monk do I call an Elder.

§41 The Two Aspects of Nibbāna

It 44

Thus was it said by the Blessed One, the Holy One. Thus have I heard:

There are, O monks, two aspects of Nibbāna: the Nibbāna-aspect with the groups of existence still remaining (*sa-upādisesa-nibbānadhātu*), and the Nibbāna-aspect with no more groups remaining (*anupādisesa-nibbānadhātu*).

But what is the Nibbāna-aspect with the groups of existence still remaining? There, O monks, the monk is an arahat. The biases have faded away in him. He has fulfilled the holy life, accomplished his task, thrown off the burden, attained his goal, cast off the fetters of existence, and is liberated through right wisdom. But there still remain with him (until his death) the five sense organs, which have not yet disappeared and through which he still experiences desirable and undesirable things, as well as bodily well-being and pain. Hence, what in such a monk is cessation of greed, hate, and delusion, this is called the Nibbāna-aspect with the groups of existence still remaining.

> For the arahat and anāgāmī no more mental suffering can arise; mental suffering, namely, is always accompanied by some degree of aversion (*dosa*) of which the arahat and anāgāmī are free forever See B. Dict.: *ariyapuggala.*

What, now, is the Nibbāna-aspect with no more groups remaining? There, O monks, the monk is an arahat ... and is liberated through right wisdom. And all those feelings, no more desired here, will (at death) come to cessation. This is called the Nibbāna-aspect with no more groups remaining.

These two Nibbāna-aspects are to be found, O monks.

Thus spoke the Blessed One. But thereafter he further said:

These two aspects of Nibbāna have been explained,
By Him, the Seer, Holy One, from clinging freed:
The one where five groups of existence still remain,
Still to be seen, though the impulse for life has ceased;
The one beyond existence, freed from life's remains,
Where all the fetters of existence are no more.
Whoso has fully understood this unborn realm,
In mind from all clinging to existence freed,
And sees the nature of all beings, happy through cessation:
This Holy One has done away with all existence.

Also this has been said. Thus have I heard.

Nibbāna (Skt. *nirvāṇa,* lit. "cessation" <*nir* + √vā>, to cease blowing, to go out) is the highest and final goal of all Buddhist striving. It is the complete cessation of all the volitional impulses of craving manifested by greed, hatred, delusion, and all forms of clinging to life. Hence, it is the final and complete deliverance from all future rebirth, old age, death, suffering and misery.

The two aspects of Nibbāna shown above are in the commentaries often called *kilesa-parinibbāna,* "cessation of defilements," and *khandha-parinibbāna,* "cessation of the groups of existence." The former aspect is realized by attaining arahatship (see. B. Dict.: *ariya-puggala*); the second one, with the death of the arahat. Thus this latter aspect consists in the coming to rest, or better said, in the "no more continuing" of the psycho-physical process of existence.

§42 The Uncreated

Ud 8:1–3

There is, O monks, a realm where there is neither earth, nor water, nor fire, nor wind, neither the sphere of boundless space, nor the sphere of boundless consciousness, nor the sphere of nothingness, nor the sphere of neither-perception-nor-non-perception (§119ff.), neither this world nor the next world, neither sun nor moon: this, O monks, I call neither a going, nor a coming, nor a standstill. Without base is it, without continuity, without support: this is the end of suffering.

> Hard is it to perceive the Deathless Realm,[1]
> Not easy is it to perceive the truth.
> Yet craving is penetrated by the Master,
> To nothing more the seer is attached.

There is, O monks, an Unborn, Unoriginated, Unformed, Uncreated. For if there were not this Unborn, Unoriginated, Unformed, Uncreated, there would be no escape possible from the born, originated, formed, created. But since, O monks, there is this Unborn, Unoriginated, Unformed, Uncreated, therefore an escape is possible from the born, originated, formed, created.

§43 The Stilled One

MN 140

Just as the oil-lamp burns conditioned by oil and wick, but after the consuming of oil and wick, and through lack of fuel, the light comes to cessation, similarly the monk knows, while experiencing a feeling endangering the body: "I experience a feeling endangering the body," and while experiencing a feeling endangering life: "I experience a feeling endangering life." And he knows: "At the dissolution of the body, and after life has been consumed, all those feelings no more desired here will become extinguished." Here the monk, thus endowed, is endowed with highest wisdom as foundation. This, indeed, is the highest and

1 *Duddasam amataṃ nāma*. The translator is of the opinion that here only *amataṃ* (the Deathless) can be the proper reading, although this is nowhere proved. The reading mostly found is *anattaṃ* which in the commentary is explained as *atta-virahitaṃ*, the not-self. Others, again, explain the word as *appamāṇaṃ*, which points to a reading *an-antaṃ*, the "Immeasurable" or the "Endless." The Siamese edition reads *anataṃ*, possibly metri causa, or through a copying error. The commentary further says that the word stands for Nibbāna, i.e. *amataṃ*. Besides, even for metrical reasons, *amataṃ* is to be preferred.

holiest wisdom, to know that all suffering has vanished. And his wisdom is founded on truth and is unshakable. What, indeed, is subject to fallibility, that is untrue; and only the infallible Nibbāna is true.

Formerly, however, when the monk was still ignorant he had performed or undertaken worldly things; these things are now overcome by him, rooted out, like a palm-tree razed to the ground, destroyed, and subject to no further coming into existence. Therefore the monk, thus endowed, is endowed with this highest renunciation as foundation. This, indeed, O monks, is the highest and holiest renunciation: the abandoning of all worldly things.[2]

Formerly, when that monk was still ignorant, he was possessed of avarice and sensual greed ... of anger, ill-will, and hatefulness ... of ignorance, delusion, and foolishness. These things are now overcome by him, rooted out, like a palm-tree razed to the ground, destroyed, and subject to no further coming into existence. Therefore the monk, thus endowed, is endowed with the highest tranquillization as foundation. This, indeed, O monks, is the highest and holiest tranquillization: the tranquillization of greed, hate, and delusion.

"I am" is an illusion. "This I am" is an illusion. "I shall be" is an illusion. "I shall not be" is an illusion. "I shall be corporeal" is an illusion. "I shall be uncorporeal" is an illusion. " I shall be endowed with perception" is an illusion. "I shall be without perception" is an illusion. "I shall be neither with nor without perception" is an illusion. Illusion is an affliction, illusion is a boil, illusion is a thorn.

If, however, all illusion is overcome, one is called a stilled one, a sage. And the stilled one, the sage, is no more

2 *Upadhi*, which has been translated here by "worldly things," may in other places be translated by "appendage, addition," substratum. This term is mostly used as a figurative expression for all kinds of passion, such as greed, clinging, views, etc., often also for the five groups of existence, for karma, even for food, possession of wives, children, landed property, herds etc., in short, for all worldly things. By the freedom from all worldly things is meant Nibbāna.

reborn, no more grows old, no more dies. That craving through which he could be reborn again no more exists. And if he is no more reborn, how can he grow old? If he no more grows old, how can he die? If he no more dies, how can he tremble? If he no more trembles, how can he still have craving?

§44 What Becomes of the Perfect One After Death?

MN 72

(The wandering ascetic Vacchagotta asks the Master:)

"Where, Master Gotama, will the Perfect One be reborn?"

I do not teach that he will be reborn.

"Then, will he not be reborn?"

Also that I do not teach.

"Then perhaps he will be reborn as well as not reborn?"

Also that I do not teach.

"Then perhaps he will be neither reborn nor not reborn?"

Also that I do not teach.

"But to all my questions, Master Gotama, you give me the same answer, that you do not teach so. I have now become bewildered and perplexed. Whatever confidence I gained by my former discussions with the Master Gotama, that has now vanished in me."

Now, enough with your bewilderment and perplexity! Profound, indeed, is this doctrine, Vaccha, difficult to perceive, difficult to understand, peace-bestowing, sublime, inaccessible to logical thinking, subtle, and only comprehensible to the wise. Hardly will you understand this doctrine without explanation, without patience, without effort. Therefore I shall question you regarding it. As you think fit, you may answer.

What do you think, Vaccha: If there is a fire burning in front of you, do you then know that there is a fire burning?

"Certainly, Master Gotama."

Now, should anybody ask you whereby that fire in front of you is kept burning, what would you answer to such a question?

"I should say that it is kept burning by means of straw and wood."

Now, suppose the fire goes out, do you then know that the fire goes out?

"Certainly, Master Gotama."

But if somebody should ask you where the extinguished fire has gone, to which direction, east, west, north, or south, what would you answer to such a question?

"That does not come into consideration, Master Gotama, because the fire that was kept going by means of straw and wood has consumed those things, and thus by not being fed by them, it has, through lack of fuel, become extinguished."

Just so, Vaccha, whatever corporeality, feeling, perception, mental formations, and consciousness there are by which one would designate the Perfect One—all that has been given up, rooted out, like a palm-tree razed to the ground, destroyed, made subject to no further coming into existence. Now liberated from corporeality, feeling, perception, mental formations, and consciousness, the Perfect One is profound, immeasurable, difficult to fathom, just like the deep ocean.

> The last words are probably to be understood in the sense of the well-known utterance of the Buddha: "He who sees the Dhamma, sees me; and he who sees me, see the Dhamma." Thus the Perfect One is the embodiment of the Dhamma and has, figuratively speaking, become one with it.

§45 **SN 44:2**

What do you think, Anurādha: are corporeality, feeling, perception, mental formations, and consciousness permanent or impermanent?

"Impermanent, O Venerable One."

But what is impermanent, is this happiness or suffering?

"Suffering, O Venerable One."

But of what is impermanent, suffering, and subject to change, can one rightly regard this as: "This belongs to me, this I am, this is my self"?

"No, O Venerable One."

Therefore, Anurādha, whatever there is of corporeality, feeling, perception, mental formations, and consciousness, whether past, present or future, one's own or outside, gross or subtle, lofty or low, far or near, these one should understand according to reality and with true wisdom: "This does not belong to me, this I am not, this is not my self."

Thus understanding, Anurādha, the noble disciple turns away from these things, and through his turning away he becomes detached, and through his being detached he is liberated, and through his being liberated the knowledge arises in him: "Liberated I am"; and he knows: "Rebirth has ceased, the holy life is fulfilled, the task is done, and nothing further remains after this."

Now, tell me, Anurādha: Do you consider corporeality as the Perfect One, or feeling, perception, mental formations, or consciousness?

"No, O Venerable One."

Or do you regard the Perfect One as contained therein?

"No, O Venerable One."

Or as outside these things?

"No, O Venerable One."

Or do you consider all these things combined as the Perfect One?

"No, O Venerable One."

Now, Anurādha, since the Perfect One is not even during his lifetime to be found according to truth and reality, can one then rightly maintain that the Perfect One will continue after death, or not continue, or continue as well as not continue, or neither continue nor not continue?

"No, O Venerable One."

Rightly so, Anurādha. Merely what suffering is, and what the cessation of suffering is: only this do I teach you, now as before.

SN 44:4

One who does not correctly perceive and understand corporeality, feeling, perception, mental formations, and consciousness, as well as their arising, cessation, and the path leading to their cessation, only he may think that the Perfect One will continue after death or not continue....

This, therefore, is the reason that the Perfect One has not answered such questions.

According to Buddhism, only the five groups of existence—or in their threefold grouping: consciousness, mental factors, and corporeality—are, in the ultimate sense (*paramattha*), considered real, though only flashing up for a moment and immediately thereafter vanishing again forever. Whenever, therefore, in the Pāli texts a "being" or "person," even the "Buddha" or the "Perfect One" or "Holy One," is spoken of, this is not said in the ultimate or highest sense, but is only to be understood as a mere conventional expression (*vohāra-vacana*). Herewith, the problem regarding the being reborn or not reborn of the Perfect One, or even of any other living being, is settled.

About rebirth, see Fund. II.

APPERTAINING TO THE FOURTH TRUTH

§46 The Two Extremes and the Middle Path

SN 56:11

Two extremes, O monks, the homeless one should not follow: he should not give himself up to indulgence in sensual pleasure, which is base, common, vulgar, unholy, unprofitable. And he also should not give himself up to self-mortification, which is painful, unholy, unprofitable. Both these extremes the Perfect One has avoided, and found the middle path, which makes one both to see and to know, which leads to peace, to discernment, to enlightenment, to Nibbāna. It is this Noble Eightfold Path, the way that leads to the cessation of suffering, namely: right understanding, right thought, right speech, right bodily action, right livelihood, right effort, right mindfulness, and right concentration.

§47 **AN 8:90**

These eight links, O monks, are to be developed for the full comprehension and penetration of greed, hate, delusion, wrath, slander, envy, stinginess, hypocrisy, cunning, stubbornness, violence, conceit, haughtiness, vanity, indolence, and for their complete annihilation, overcoming, vanishing, cessation, abandoning, destruction, renunciation, and the detachment therefrom.

Dhp 274–76

This is the only path that leads
To purity of understanding.
If you pursue this eightfold path,
Then Māra will be blinded soon.

And if you walk along this path,
Then you will put an end to pain.
I found the path and understood
How one is freed from pricking bane.

You have to struggle hard yourselves,
The Buddhas only point the way.
Who follows it with mind absorbed,
Will find release from Māra's sway.

Pāli *māra,* lit. murderer, death (probably connected with Norse *mara,* Germ. *mahr,* Engl. night*mare,* Lat. *mors,* etc.), is the "Tempter," i.e. the personification of the objects of sensual desire. "You should overcome the longing concerning Māra. But what is Māra? Corporeality is Māra; the longing for it you should overcome. Feeling ... Perception ... Mental formations ... Consciousness is Māra; the longing for it you should overcome" (SN 23:35). In other texts, Māra is said to be everything impermanent, miserable, impersonal, passing, and vanishing. See. B. Dict.

§48 **Right Understanding**

AN 10:121

Just as, O monks, the dawn is the forerunner and first indication of the rising of the sun, just so, O monks, right understanding is the forerunner and first indication of wholesome things.

§49 To the Kālāmas

AN 3:65

Do not go, O Kālāmas, by mere hearsay, tradition, or rumours, nor by the texts handed down, by mere reasoning and logical deduction, nor by external considerations; and do not believe a thing because it agrees with your fancies and speculations, or with another's seeming ability or because the monk that tells it is your master.

What do you think: do greed, hate, and delusion that arise in a person lead him to blessing or misfortune?

"To misfortune, O Venerable One."

Out of greed, hate, and delusion, overwhelmed by greed, hate, and delusion, one destroys life, takes others' property, has intercourse with one's neighbour's wife, speaks untruth, and one also induces others to such things, which leads for a long time to one's misery and suffering.

"Thus it is, O Venerable One."

What do you think: are these things wholesome or unwholesome?

"Unwholesome, O Venerable One."

Reprehensible or blameless?

"Reprehensible, O Venerable One."

Are they praised or blamed by the wise?

"Blamed, O Venerable One."

And do these things, undertaken and carried out, lead to misfortune or suffering, or not; or how do you think about it?

"They lead to misfortune and suffering, thus we think."

What do you think, O Kālāmas: do greedlessness, hatelessness, and undeludedness that arise in a person, lead him to blessing or misfortune?

"To blessing, O Venerable One."

Freed from greed, hate, and delusion, not overwhelmed by greed, hate, and delusion, one does not destroy life, nor take others' property, nor have intercourse with one's neighbour's wife, nor speak untruth; and one also induces others to such things, which leads for a long time to one's blessing and happiness.

"Thus it is, O Venerable One."

What do you think: are these things wholesome or unwholesome?

"Wholesome, O Venerable One."

Reprehensible or blameless?

"Blameless, O Venerable One."

Are they praised or blamed by the wise?

"Praised, O Venerable One."

And do these things, undertaken and carried out, lead to blessing and happiness, or not, or how do you think about it?

"They lead to blessing and happiness, thus we think."

Thus, O Kālāmas, with a mind freed from greed and ill-will, undefiled, purified, the noble disciple is already during life assured of a fourfold consolation: "If there is another world, and a fruit and result of wholesome and unwholesome actions (kamma), then it may be that, at the dissolution of the body, after death, I shall be reborn in a happy sphere, a heavenly world." Of this first consolation he is assured.

"And if there is no other world, no fruit and result of wholesome and unwholesome actions, then I live at least here, in this world, an untroubled and happy life, free from hate and ill-will." Of this second consolation he is assured.

"And if evil things befall evildoers—but I do not harbour ill-will against anyone—how can I, who am doing no evil, meet with evil things?" Of this third consolation he is assured.

"And if no evil things befall evildoers, then I know myself in both ways pure." Of this fourth consolation he is assured.

§50 MN 43

There are, O brothers, two conditions for the arising of right understanding, namely: instruction through another person, and one's own wise consideration.

§51 AN 1:17.9

If, O monks, *nimba* seed, or *kosātaki* seed, or the seed of the bitter pumpkin is sown on wet ground, then all the solid and liquid substances which it absorbs will get a bitter and repulsive taste. And why? Because the seed is bitter. Just so, O monks, whatever a man, led by wrong views, carries out and undertakes, and whatever he thinks and whatever he strives for, whatever his longings and inclinations are, all this will lead him to an undesired, unpleasant, disagreeable state, to misfortune and suffering. And why? Because his views are evil.

§52 AN 1:15.1–8

It is impossible, O monks, and unfounded that someone possessed of right understanding should consider any formation of existence as permanent ... any formation of existence as real happiness ... anything whatever as a real self. But it is possible that the worldling may have such a belief.

It is impossible and unfounded that someone possessed of right understanding should deprive his mother of life ... should deprive his father of life ... should deprive an arahat of life ... should, with wicked mind, shed the blood of a Perfect One ... should cause a schism in the Order of Monks. But it is possible that the worldling may commit such an act.

The aforementioned five crimes, matricide, parricide, etc., are called "acts with immediate results," i.e. deeds that after death lead immediately to hell. See B. Dict.: *ānantarika kamma.*

§53 Right Thought, Right Speech, Right Action (The Ten Courses of Wholesome Karma)

AN 10:176

Threefold, Cunda, is purity of bodily action, fourfold of speech, threefold of mind.

But how, Cunda, is purity of bodily action threefold?

(1) Herein, someone avoids the destruction of life, abstains from killing living beings. Without stick or sword,

conscientious, full of sympathy, he is anxious for the welfare of living beings.

(2) He avoids stealing, abstains from it; what another person possesses of goods and chattel in the village or in the wood, that he does not take away with thievish intent.

(3) He avoids unlawful sexual intercourse, abstains from it. He has no intercourse with such persons as are still under the protection of father, mother, brother, sister, or relatives, nor with married women nor female convicts, nor, lastly, with betrothed girls.

But how, Cunda, is purity of speech fourfold?

(1) Herein, someone avoids lying, abstains from lying. He speaks the truth, is devoted to the truth, reliable, worthy of confidence, not a deceiver of others. Being at a meeting or amongst people, or in the midst of his relatives, or in a society, or in the king's court, and called upon and asked as witness to tell what he knows, he answers, if he knows nothing: "I know nothing"; and if he knows, he answers: "I know." If he has seen nothing, he answers: "I have seen nothing"; and if he has seen, he answers: "I have seen." Thus he never knowingly speaks a lie, neither for the sake of his own advantage, nor for the sake of another person's advantage, nor for the sake of any advantage whatsoever.

(2) He avoids tale-bearing, abstains from tale-bearing. What he has heard here, he does not repeat there so as to cause dissension there; and what he has heard there, he does not repeat here so as to cause dissension here. Thus he unites those who are divided; and those who are united, he encourages. Concord gladdens him, he delights and rejoices in concord; and it is concord that he spreads by his words.

(3) He avoids harsh language, abstains from harsh language. He speaks such words as are gentle, soothing to the ear, loving, going to the heart, courteous, dear, and agreeable.

(4) He avoids vain talk, abstains from vain talk. He speaks at the right time, in accordance with facts, speaks what is useful, speaks about the doctrine and the discipline; his

speech is like a treasure, uttered at the right moment, accompanied by arguments, moderate, and full of sense.

But how, Cunda, is purity of mind threefold?

(1) Herein, someone is without avarice. Whatever another person possesses of goods and chattel, he does not long for it: "Oh, that I might get what the other person possesses!"

(2) He is free from ill-will, harbours no evil thoughts in his mind; and he thinks: "Oh, may these beings be free from hatred and ill-will, and may they lead a happy life free from trouble!"

(3) He possesses right understanding and the unshakable view: "Gifts, donations, and offerings are not worthless. There is a fruit and result of wholesome and unwholesome action (*kamma*). There is this world, and there is the next world. There are (duties towards) father and mother; there are spontaneously reborn beings. There are in this world monks and brahmins of right and perfect life, who have themselves understood and realized both this world and the next, and are able to explain them both."

These, Cunda, are the ten courses of wholesome action.

§54 Avoiding Vulgar Speech

SN 56:10

Do not, O monks, give yourselves up to manifold vulgar talk, such as: talk about kings, robbers, ministers, armies, dangers, wars, food and drink, clothes and dwellings, garlands and perfumes, relations, conveyances, villages, hamlets, towns and countries, women and heroes, street-talk and well-talk, talk about ghosts of ancestors, gossip, talk about land and sea, about gain and loss.

> In the commentaries four further vulgar, lit. "beastly," subjects of talk are enumerated, so that the number is raised from 28 to 32, namely: talk about sensual pleasures and self-mortification, eternity and annihilation.

And why, O monks, should you not give yourselves up to such talk? Because such talk is senseless, unsuited to the genuine holy life, and does not lead to aversion, detachment, cessation, peace, penetration, enlightenment, and Nibbāna.

If you wish to speak together, you may speak about the truth of suffering, about its origination, its cessation, and the path leading to its cessation. And why? Because such talk is fraught with meaning, suited to the genuine holy life, and leads to aversion, detachment, cessation, peace, penetration, enlightenment, and Nibbāna.

§55 Right Effort

AN 4:14

There are four efforts, O monks: the effort to avoid, the effort to overcome, the effort to develop, and the effort to maintain.

(1) But what, O monks, is the effort to avoid? In this case, when perceiving a form with the eye, a sound with the ear, an odour with the nose, a taste with the tongue, an impression with the body, an object with the mind, the monk neither adheres to the whole nor to its parts. And he strives to ward off that through which evil and unwholesome states, greed and sorrow, would arise if he remained with unguarded senses; and he watches over his senses, restrains his senses. This is called the effort to avoid.

(2) But what, O monks, is the effort to overcome? In this case, the monk does not retain any thought of sensual lust, ill-will, or grief, or any other evil and unwholesome states that may have arisen; he abandons them, dispels them, destroys them, causes them to disappear. This is called the effort to overcome.

(3) But what, O monks, is the effort to develop? In this case, the monk develops the factors of enlightenment, bent on solitude, on detachment, on cessation, and ending in deliverance, namely: mindfulness (*sati*), investigation of phenomena (*dhamma-vicaya*), energy (*viriya*), rapture (*pīti*), tranquillity (*passaddhi*), concentration (*samādhi*), and equanimity (*upekkhā*). This is called the effort to develop.

(4) But what, O monks, is the effort to maintain? In this case, the monk keeps firmly in his mind a favourable object of concentration that has arisen, such as the mental image of a skeleton, of a corpse infested by worms, of a corpse blue-black in colour, of a festering corpse, of a corpse riddled with holes, of a corpse swollen up. This is called the effort to maintain.

These, O monks, are the four efforts.

§56 **Right Concentration**

MN 44

Fixing the mind to one single object (*citt' ekaggatā*, lit. "one-pointedness of mind"): this is concentration.

The four applications of mindfulness (7th step) are the objects of concentration.

The four great efforts (6th step) are the requisites for concentration.

The practising, developing, and cultivating of these things is the development (*bhāvanā*) of concentration.

§57 SN 22:5

Develop your concentration, O monks, for one who has concentration understands things according to reality. And what are these things? The arising and passing of corporeality, feeling, perception, mental formations, and consciousness.

On the nature of the Eightfold Path, see B. Dict.: *magga.*

THREEFOLD DIVISION OF THE PATH

For any real progress and the attainment of the supramundane paths of the sotāpanna, etc. (see B. Dict.: *ariya-puggala*), right understanding forms the absolutely necessary foundation: for which reason, too, right understanding is given at the beginning of the Noble Eightfold Path. With regard to the gradual development and the attaining of highest perfection in each of the eight links, however, its threefold division into morality, concentration, and wisdom (mentioned at the beginning) comes into consideration, as it is said:

§58 AN 5:22

O monks, without having mastered the domain of morality (*sīla*), it is not possible to master the domain of concentration (*samādhi*). Without having mastered the domain of concentration, it is not possible to master the domain of wisdom (*paññā*).

§59 DN 16 (iv)

It is through not understanding, not penetrating four things, O monks, that I as well as you had to wander so long through this round of rebirths. And these four things are: noble morality, noble concentration, noble wisdom, and noble deliverance. Now, however, O monks, noble morality, concentration, wisdom, and deliverance have been understood and penetrated, the thirst for existence has been cut off, the stream of life has vanished, and no further rebirth is to be expected.

Morality and concentration
And wisdom and deliverance:
These things were fully penetrated
By Him, the glorious Gotama.

And having understood the Dhamma,
The Buddha showed it to the monks,
The pain-destroyer, He our Master,
The Seer, freed from vanity.

§60 The Threefold Training

AN 3:88, 89

There are, O monks, three kinds of training: training in higher morality (*adhisīla-sikkhā*), training in higher consciousness (*adhicitta-sikkhā*), training in higher wisdom (*adhipaññā-sikkhā*).

(1) But what, O monks, is the training in higher morality? Herein the monk is possessed of morality, is restrained with regard to the monk's rules, perfect in conduct and behaviour and, abhorring the least offences, trains himself in the moral rules he has undertaken. This is called the training in higher morality.

(2) But what, O monks, is the training in higher consciousness? Herein the monk, detached from sensuous objects, detached from karmically unwholesome states, enters into the first ... the second ... the third ... the fourth absorption (*jhāna*).

(3) But what, O monks, is the training in higher wisdom? Herein the monk understands according to reality what suffering is, what the origination of suffering is, what the cessation of suffering is, and what the path is leading to the cessation of suffering.

§61 MN 6

If, O monks, the monk wishes: "Oh, that I may be able, after the vanishing of all taints, already during life to perceive the deliverance of mind, the deliverance through wisdom, realize it and make it my own!"—then he should practise perfect morality, be devoted to mental tranquillity (*samatha*), not neglect the mental absorptions, be possessed of insight (*vipassanā*), and frequent lonely places.

§62 The Path in its Threefold Division

MN 44

"Are, O Venerable Dhammadinnā, the three domains (morality, concentration, wisdom) included in the Noble Eightfold Path, or is the Noble Eightfold Path included in the three domains?"

"The three domains, Visākha (the former husband of the nun Dhammadinnā), are not included in the Noble Eightfold Path, but the Noble Eightfold Path is included in the three domains. Right speech, right bodily action, and right livelihood: these things are included in the domain of morality (*sīlakkhandha*). Right effort, right mindfulness, and right concentration: these things are included in the domain of concentration (*samādhikkhandha*). Right understanding and right thought: these things are included in the domain of wisdom (*paññākkhandha*)."

The domain of *sīla*, for instance, comprises also all the regulations of the monk's Code of Discipline (*Vinaya*), and for the layman, accepted rules of behaviour, etc.; while the *sīla* of the Noble Eightfold Path refers to morality in the strict sense and consists of fourfold right speech, threefold right bodily action, and a pure way of livelihood (see §1). Also the range of the other two domains is wider than the corresponding divisions of the Eightfold Path.

§63 The seven stages of purity
(satta-visuddhi)

The development of the Noble Eightfold Path—or more correctly, the gradual purification and perfection of morality, concentration, and wisdom—is accomplished by way of the seven stages of purity. They are:

(1) purity of morality (*sīla-visuddhi*),
(2) purity of mind (*citta-visuddhi*),
(3) purity of understanding (*diṭṭhi-visuddhi*),
(4) purity of escaping doubt (*kaṅkhāvītaraṇa- visuddhi*),
(5) purity of the knowledge and vision regarding path and not-path (*maggāmagga-ñāṇadassana-visuddhi*),
(6) purity of the knowledge and vision of progress (*paṭipadā-ñāṇadassana-visuddhi*),
(7) purity of knowledge and vision (*ñāṇadassana-visuddhi*).

The only place in the Canon where the seven stages of purity are not only enumerated but also illustrated by a simile, is the discourse on the Simile of the Stagecoaches (MN 24). In DN 34 the seven stages are only enumerated and called "the seven things to be developed."

§64 The Simile of the Seven Stagecoaches
MN 24

The Venerable Sāriputta spoke to the Venerable Puṇṇa, the son of Mantāni, thus:

"We are leading, O brother, the holy life under the Blessed One."

"Yes, brother."

"Now, brother is it for purity of morality that one leads the holy life under the Blessed One?"

"No, brother."

"Or for purity of mind?"

"No, brother."

"Or for purity of understanding?"

"No, brother."

"Or for purity of escape from doubt?"

"No, brother."

"Or for purity of the knowledge and vision regarding path and not-path?"

"No, brother."

"Or for purity of knowledge and vision of progress?"

"No, brother."

"Or for purity of knowledge and vision?"

"No, brother."

"But how is it, brother? To all my questions you answer: 'No, brother.' But for the sake of what does one really lead the holy life under the Blessed One?"

"One leads the holy life under the Blessed One for the sake of the perfect Nibbāna free from clinging, O brother."

"Then, O brother, is purity of morality the same as the perfect Nibbāna free from clinging?"

"No, brother."

"Or purity of mind?"

"No, brother."

"Or purity of understanding ... or of escape from doubt ... or of the knowledge and vision regarding path and not-path ... or of the knowledge and vision of progress ... or of knowledge and vision?"

"No, brother."

"But how, brother, are we to understand the meaning of these words?"

"If, O brother, the Blessed One had explained the purity of morality ... or of understanding ... or of escape from doubt, etc., as the perfect Nibbāna free from clinging, in that case he would have explained something bound up with clinging as perfect Nibbāna free from clinging.

"If, however, the realization of the perfect Nibbāna free from clinging were independent of these things, in that case even the worldling could attain Nibbāna. For the worldling is without these things. Thus I shall give you a simile, for also through a simile an intelligent man may understand the meaning.

"Let us say, O brother, Pasenadi, the Kosala king, while staying at Sāvatthī had some urgent matter to settle in Sāketa, and seven stagecoaches between Sāvatthī and Sāketa were kept ready for him. And Pasenadi, the Kosala king, stepped out through the palace gate and mounted the first stagecoach and travelled by it up to the second stagecoach. Then he sent back the first stagecoach, mounted the second, and travelled by it up to the third stagecoach ... the fourth ... the fifth ... the sixth. Then he sent back the sixth stagecoach, mounted the seventh, and travelled by it up to the palace gate of Sāketa.

"Now, suppose the king, while in the palace, were asked by his friends, cousins, and blood-relations whether he had come by this coach from Sāvatthī up to the palace gate at Sāketa. Now, what would be the right answer for Pasenadi, the Kosala king?"

"He would rightly answer thus: 'While I was staying at Sāvatthī, I had to settle an urgent matter in Sāketa. Therefore, between Sāvatthī and Sāketa, seven stagecoaches were kept ready for me. So I stepped out through the palace gate at Sāvatthī, mounted the first stagecoach and travelled by it up to the second stagecoach. Then I sent back the first stagecoach, mounted the second, and travelled by it up to the third stagecoach ... by the third up to the fourth ... by the fourth up to the fifth ... by the fifth up to the sixth. Then I sent back the sixth stagecoach, mounted the seventh, and travelled by it up to the palace gate at Sāketa.' With such an explanation Pasenadi, the Kosala king, would give the right answer."

"Just so, O brother, purity of morality has only purity of mind as goal, purity of mind only purity of understanding, purity of understanding only purity of escape from doubt, purity of escape from doubt only purity of the knowledge and vision regarding path and not-path, purity of the knowledge and vision regarding path and not-path only purity of the knowledge and vision of progress, purity of the knowledge and vision of progress only purity of knowledge and vision. Purity of knowledge and vision, however, has as goal the perfect Nibbāna free from clinging. And for the sake of the perfect Nibbāna free from clinging, O brother, one leads the holy life under the Blessed One."

1

Morality

(*sīla*)

1
Morality
(*sīla*)

GENERAL REMARKS

§65 Morality (*sīla*) is the state of volition and mind manifested in right action and right speech, and not merely the external bodily and verbal manifestations, which have to be considered only as physical phenomena.

Moreover, morality is not, as it may appear from the negative expressions in the Suttas (such as "abstaining" from killing, stealing, etc.), something negative or passive, consisting merely in "not producing evil manifestations." It is, quite to the contrary, the intentional restraint based on the simultaneous arising of a noble state of volition and mind.

The morality of the Noble Eightfold Path is the true or "natural morality" (*pakati-sīla*), in contradistinction to "prescribed rules" (*paṇṇatti-sīla*).

The five moral rules (*pañca-sīla*) binding on all Buddhists are: abstaining from killing, stealing, unlawful sexual intercourse, lying, and intoxicants.

The ten precepts (*dasa-sīla*), which are binding on all novices and monks, are: (1) abstaining from killing, (2) from stealing, (3) from unchastity, (4) from lying, (5) from intoxicants, (6) from eating after noon, (7) from dance, song, music, and shows, (8) from garlands, perfumes, cosmetics, etc., (9) from high and luxurious couches, (10) from accepting gold and silver.

In the case of the eight precepts (*aṭṭha-sīla*), which many devotees observe on full-moon, new-moon, the first and last quarter of the moon, the so-called "fasting days" (*uposatha*)—the seventh and eighth of the aforementioned ten precepts are here combined in the seventh precept, while the ninth becomes the eighth.

§66 The Five Moral Precepts

AN 5:174

(The Blessed One to Anāthapiṇḍika:)

Whoever, O householder, has not overcome five terrible evils, such a one is without morality and will be reborn in hell. And what are those five terrible evils? They are killing, stealing, unlawful sexual intercourse, lying, and taking intoxicants. But whoever has overcome these five terrible evils, such a one is virtuous and will be reborn in a happy world.

Now just as one who is committing these things produces present and future terrible misery, and experiences mental pain and grief, just so one who abstains from these things produces neither present nor future terrible misery, nor does he experience mental pain and grief. Such terrible evil is extinguished in him.

Whoever murders living beings,
Speaks words that are not true,
Takes what does not belong to him,
Seduces wives of other men,
And drinks intoxicating drinks,
To which he ever strongly clings:
A man who does not shun these evils,
Has no morality indeed;
And when his body once dissolves,
That fool will fall to deepest hell.

Who does no harm to anyone,
Who never utters any lie,
Who never takes what is not his,
Nor seduces his neighbour's wife,
Nor ever wishes in all his life
To drink intoxicating drinks:
A man who shuns these five evils
Is rightly called a virtuous man;
And when his body once dissolves,
This wise man rises heavenward.

§67 Meat-Eating

Though Buddhism condemns the destruction of animal life as a thoroughly evil and immoral act, it nevertheless does not hold the belief that under all circumstances the eating of meat is an immoral act. The karmical quality of any act depends on the underlying volition (*cetanā*) and cannot be called either karmically wholesome (*kusala*) or unwholesome (*akusala*) apart from the volition. Thus the act of meat-eating as such is morally indeterminate.

MN 55

Under three conditions, I say, is meat-eating to be rejected: if one has seen, heard, or suspected (that the animal concerned has been killed especially for oneself).

> One who partakes of meat under these conditions would thereby, as it were, approve the killing of animals and support the slaughterer in his cruel work. The fact, on the other hand, that even the Buddha himself has sometimes eaten meat, is proved by many passages in the Canon (e.g. AN 5:44; 8:12, etc.). It is further reported in the Vinaya that the Buddha categorically rejected Devadatta's proposal to forbid meat-eating to the monks. And that monks were normally allowed to eat meat may be already inferred from the Vinaya rule which forbids ten kinds of meat—but for merely external reasons—such as that of a tiger, a snake, an elephant, etc. (B. Dict.).

DN 31

The partaking of intoxicating and inebriating drinks such as wine and liquor brings sixfold misfortune: it leads to the loss of one's property, to quarrels, is a source of sickness, creates a bad reputation, destroys the sense of moral shame, and weakens the intelligence.

§68 The Eight Precepts

AN 8:44

The observance of the observance day endowed with eight features brings high reward and blessing, is of sublime dignity and greatness. And which are these eight features? Here, the noble disciple considers within himself: (1) "Throughout life the arahats avoid the killing of living beings, abstain from hurting them. Without cudgel or weapon, tender-hearted, full of kindness, they think of the welfare of all living beings and creatures. And also I, this day and night, avoid the killing and hurting of living beings. Without cudgel or weapon, tender-hearted, full of kindness, I think of the welfare of all living beings and creatures. In this regard I follow the arahats, and I shall have observed the observance day." With this first feature is the observance day endowed.

(2) "Throughout life the arahats avoid the stealing of others' property and abstain from stealing. Waiting till a thing is given, free from thievish intent, they remain pure in heart. And also I, this day and night, avoid stealing and abstain from it. In this regard, I follow the arahats, and I shall have observed the observance day." With this second feature is the observance day endowed.

(3) "Throughout life the arahats avoid unchastity, living chaste, keeping aloof, away from sexual intercourse, the vulgar practice. And also I, this day and night, avoid unchastity, living chaste, keeping aloof, away from sexual intercourse, the vulgar practice. In this regard I follow the arahats, and I shall have observed the observance day." With this third feature is the observance day endowed.

(4) "Throughout life the arahats avoid lying and abstain therefrom; they speak the truth, are devoted to the truth, reliable, worthy of confidence, not deceivers of people. And also I, this day and night, avoid lying and abstain therefrom; I speak the truth, am devoted to the truth, worthy of confidence, not a deceiver of people. In this regard I follow the arahats, and I shall have observed the observance day." With this fourth feature is the observance day endowed.

(5) "Throughout life the arahats avoid intoxicating drinks, such as wine and liquor, and abstain therefrom. And also I, this day and night, avoid intoxicating drinks and abstain

therefrom. In this regard I follow the arahats, and I shall have observed the observance day." With this fifth feature is the observance day endowed.

(6) "Throughout life the arahats eat only at one time of the day (forenoon), abstaining from food at night, not eating at improper hours. And also I, this day and night, shall not eat at improper hours. In this regard I follow the arahats, and I shall have observed the observance day." With this sixth feature is the observance day endowed.

(7) "Throughout life the arahats keep aloof from dance, song, music, and shows; they reject garlands, perfumes, ointment, as well as any kind of adornment and cosmetics. And also I, this day and night, shall keep aloof from dance, song, music, shows, reject garlands, perfumes, ointment, as well as any kind of adornment and cosmetics. In this regard I follow the arahats, and I shall have observed the observance day." With this seventh feature is the observance day endowed.

(8) "Throughout life the arahats avoid high and luxurious couches, using only a low couch, be it a bed or a layer of straw. And also I, this day and night, shall avoid high and luxurious couches, using only a low couch, be it a bed or a layer of straw. In this regard I follow the arahats, and I shall have observed the observance day." With this eighth feature is the observance day endowed.

Observed in this way, the observance day endowed with eight features brings high reward and blessing, is of sublime dignity and greatness.

§69 The Blessing of Morality

AN 10:1

"What, O Venerable One, is the reward and blessing of wholesome morality?"

Freedom from remorse, Ānanda.

"And of freedom from remorse?"

Joy, Ānanda.

"And of joy?"

Rapture, Ānanda.

"And of rapture?"
Tranquillity, Ānanda.
"And of tranquillity?"
Happiness, Ānanda.
"And of happiness?"
Concentration, Ānanda.
"And of concentration?"
Vision and knowledge according to reality.
"And of the vision and knowledge according to reality?"
Turning away and detachment, Ānanda.
"And of turning away and detachment?"

The vision and knowledge with regard to deliverance, Ānanda. Thus, the reward and fruit of wholesome morality is freedom from remorse; the reward of freedom from remorse, joy; of joy, rapture; of rapture, tranquillity; of tranquillity, happiness; of happiness, concentration; of concentration, the vision and knowledge according to reality; of the vision and knowledge according to reality, turning away and detachment; of turning away and detachment; the vision and knowledge with regard to deliverance.

Thus, Ānanda, wholesome morality leads step by step to the highest.

§70 The Monk of Moral Perfection

DN 2

How is a monk perfect in morality?

Herein the monk avoids the destroying of life ... stealing ... unchastity ... lying ... tale-bearing ... harsh language ... frivolous talk ... avoids the destruction of seeds and plant life ... eats only at one time of the day ... keeps aloof from dance, song, music, and shows ... rejects garlands, perfumes, ointment, as well as any kind of adornment and cosmetics ... avoids high and gorgeous couches ... does not accept gold and silver ... nor women or girls ... owns no male or female slaves; no goats, sheep, fowls, pigs, elephants, cows or horses; no land and goods; does not go on errands and do the duties of a messenger; keeps aloof from buying and selling things; has nothing to do with false measures, metals, and weights; avoids the crooked ways of bribery, deception, and fraud; keeps aloof from stabbing, beating, chaining, attacking, plundering, and oppressing.... He does not hoard up things (as robes, food, etc.) ... does not gain his livelihood by such vulgar arts as fortune-telling.... This is his morality. And endowed with this noble morality he experiences in his heart a blameless happiness. In such a way is the monk perfect in morality.

§71

I. Purity of Morality
(*sīla-visuddhi*)

This term comprises the four kinds of moral purity (*cātu-pārisuddhi-sīla*), which are found and explained separately in the Suttas, and which refer to the morality of the monk. They are:

(1) Morality consisting in restraint with regard to the moral code of the Order (*pātimokkha-saṃvara-sīla*).
(2) Morality consisting in restraint of the senses (*indriya-saṃvara-sīla*).
(3) Morality consisting in purity of livelihood (*ājīva-pārisuddhi-sīla*).
(4) Morality regarding the four requisites (*paccaya-sannissita-sīla*). A detailed explanation is given in Vism I 42–130.

MN 53

(1) Herein, Mahānāma, the noble disciple is perfect in restraint with regard to the moral code of the monks (*pātimokkha*), perfect in conduct and behaviour, and seeing danger in the minutest offences, he trains himself in the moral rules taken upon himself.

(2) Now, Mahānāma, in perceiving a visible object with the eye ... a sound with the ear ... an odour with the nose ... a taste with the tongue ... an impression with the body ... an object with the mind, the noble disciple clings neither to the whole nor its details, and he tries to ward off that which, on his being unguarded in his senses, might give rise

to evil and unwholesome states, to greed and sorrow. And he watches over his senses, keeps his senses under control.

DN 2

(3) Now certain monks and brahmins, after eating the food that has been offered to them in faith, undertake to go on errands and deliver messages ... or they gain their livelihood through fraud, persuasion, hints, backbiting, or through hunting after ever greater and greater gain, or through low arts of prophesying etc. ... from all such wrong ways of gaining one's livelihood he keeps away.

(4a) Herein, O monks, the monk, wisely reflecting, puts on his robes (*cīvara*) only for warding off heat and cold, as well as molestation by gnats, mosquitoes, wind, sun, and creeping things, or for the covering of the private parts.

(4b) Wisely reflecting, he takes his almsfood (*piṇḍapāta*) neither for amusement, nor vanity, nor to become handsome and graceful, but only for the maintenance and upkeep of this body, to prevent harm, and to support the holy life, thinking: "In this way I shall put an end to former feelings (hunger, etc.) and not allow new feelings (bodily complaints) to arise, and I shall be assured of long life, blamelessness, and happiness."

(4c) Wisely reflecting, he uses his dwelling place (*senāsana*) only for warding off heat and cold, as well as molestation by gnats, mosquitoes, wind, sun and creeping things, only to ward off the danger of bad weather and to enjoy solitude.

(4d) Wisely reflecting, he uses remedies (*gilānapaccaya*) and medicines, only to get rid of feelings of sickness, and for the sake of the highest state free from suffering.

§72 The Ascetical Means of Purification (*dhutaṅga*)

Dhutaṅga, according to Vism II, 2ff., lit. "means of shaking off," is the name for certain ascetical vows or practices intended to strengthen frugality, renunciation, energy, etc. Of these vows either one or several may be taken up for a longer or shorter period of time. For details see Vism and B. Dict.

AN 5:181–90

Of five kinds, O monks, are the forest monks, the wearers of patched-up robes, the monks living at the foot of trees, the cemetery monks, the open-air monks, the ever-sitters, the monks contented with any sleeping place, the monks eating at one sitting, the monks refusing any later meal, the monks eating from only one bowl. And what are these five kinds?

There are those that observe these practices through stupidity and foolishness; those that observe them with evil intention and greedy mind; those that observe them through craziness and mental derangement; those that observe them because they have been praised by the Buddha and his disciples; those that observe them for the sake of frugality, contentedness, austerity, detachment, just for the sake of the worth of this mode of living. And those that observe the practices for the sake of frugality, contentedness, austerity, detachment, just for the sake of the worth of this mode of living—they are the highest, the best, foremost, most excellent and distinguished among those five kinds of monks.

AN 1:20.1

Certainly, O monks, it is of great advantage to live in the forest, to go for alms, to wear patched-up robes, to be satisfied with only three robes.

MN 113

Here, O monks, a certain monk lives as a hermit in the forest and thinks thus: "I am indeed a forest hermit, but the others do not live in the forest." And on account of his living in the forest, he prides himself and looks down on others. This, O monks, is the way of a bad man.

The good man, however, considers thus: "Not through my living in the forest do the greedy, hateful, and deluded states of the mind come to disappear. Even if one does

2
Concentration
(*samādhi*)

2
Concentration
(*samādhi*)

II. PURITY OF MIND
(*citta-visuddhi*)

General Remarks

§73 Here, by concentration, not merely the eighth link of the Noble Eightfold Path is meant, but the training in higher mentality consisting of the sixth, seventh, and eighth links. In other words, what is here called concentration (*samādhi*), or purity of mind, refers to the entire domain of mental and spiritual development, called in Pāli *bhāvanā* (see below). About the three domains of morality, concentration, and wisdom, see §I and §60.

The term *samādhi* literally means "being firmly put together" <*sam* + *ā* + √*dhā*> and is explained in the Suttas as a state of mind directed to a single object (*citt'ekaggatā*, lit. "one-pointedness of mind"). If the term is taken in its widest sense, a certain degree of mental concentration is inseparably associated with any state of consciousness whatever; it is one of the seven inseparable mental factors of consciousness.

Right concentration (*sammā-samādhi*) is associated with all karmically wholesome consciousness, while wrong concentration (*micchā-samādhi*) is associated with all karmically unwholesome consciousness. Whenever the term "concentration" is used, it refers to "right concentration."

The commentaries distinguish three stages in concentration:

1. preliminary concentration (*parikamma-samādhi*),
2. neighbourhood concentration (*upacāra-samādhi*),
3. absorption concentration (*appanā-samādhi*).

See Fund. IV.

§74 *Bhāvanā* is derived from the causative form of the verbal root *bhū, bhavati*, "to be, to become." Literally it means: the "causing to be, or to become," the calling into existence, unfolding or development. By Western scholars it is commonly, but not quite appropriately, translated by the word "meditation."

There are two kinds of mental development: development of mental tranquillity (*samatha-bhāvanā*) or of concentration (*samādhi-bhāvanā*); and development of insight (*vipassanā-bhāvanā*) or of wisdom (*paññā-bhāvanā*). Both terms, mental tranquillity and insight, occur very often in the Suttas.

Tranquillity (*samatha*) is the unshaken, peaceful, and lucid state of mind attained in the meditative absorptions (*jhāna*; see §76). Insight (*vipassanā*), however, is the penetrative understanding, by direct meditative experience, of the impermanence, unsatisfactoriness, and selflessness (*anicca, dukkha, anattā*) of all corporeal and mental phenomena of existence, i.e. the all-inclusive five groups (*khandha*) of existence, namely: corporeality, feeling, perception, mental formations, and consciousness.

Mental tranquillity, according to the commentary Saṅkhepa-vaṇṇanā, bestows a threefold blessing: favourable rebirth, happy life, and mental purity suitable for gaining insight. Concentration, in fact, forms the necessary foundation and preliminary condition for insight by freeing the mind from impurities and mental obstacles. Insight, however, is that which may lead immediately to entrance into one of the four supermundane stages of holiness (see B. Dict.: *ariya-puggala*). In Mil. it is said: "Just as, by bringing a lighted lamp into a dark chamber, the darkness is dispelled, brightness is produced, and light spreads out, so that all the objects become visible, just so does insight, whenever it arises, dispel the darkness of ignorance and produce the light of wisdom."

§75 Forty Concentration Exercises

There are forty concentration exercises (*kammaṭṭhāna*) leading to the tranquillity of the absorptions. They are:

I. Ten *kasiṇa* exercises: (1) earth *kasiṇa*, (2) water *kasiṇa*, (3) fire *kasiṇa*, (4) wind *kasiṇa*, (5) blue *kasiṇa*, (6) yellow *kasiṇa*, (7) red *kasiṇa*, (8) white *kasiṇa*, (9) light *kasiṇa*, (10) space *kasiṇa*. The older suttas replace the light *kasiṇa* with the consciousness *kasiṇa*, as at AN 10:29.

II. Ten perceptions of loathsomeness (*asubha-saññā*): a swollen-up corpse, a bluish discoloured corpse, a festering corpse, a split corpse, a gnawed corpse, a scattered corpse, a dismembered and scattered corpse, a blood-stained corpse, a corpse full of worms, a skeleton. More or less identical with these exercises are the nine cemetery contemplations in MN 10 and DN 22, and the contemplation in AN 4:14, quoted below.

III. Ten contemplations (*anussati*): (1) on the Buddha, (2) the Doctrine, (3) the Community of Noble Disciples, (4) morality, (5) liberality, (6) heavenly beings, (7) death, (8) body, (9) in-and-out-breathing, (10) peace.

While 1–6 are mostly explained in one and the same sutta, (7)–(10) are described each separately in different suttas, e.g. (7) in AN 8:73f. (8) in MN 119 (but not as in MN 10, while in Vism the meditation refers to the thirty-two parts of the body); (9) in MN 118; (10) in AN 9:52–61, 10:26.

IV. Four divine abodes (*brahma-vihāra*): (1) all-embracing kindness (*mettā*), (2) compassion (*karuṇā*), (3) altruistic joy (*muditā*)), (4) equanimity (*upekkhā*).

V. Four immaterial spheres (*arūpāyatana*): (1) sphere of boundless space, (2) sphere of boundless consciousness, (3) sphere of nothingness, (4) sphere of neither-perception-nor-non-perception.

VI. Perception of the loathsomeness of food.

VII. Analysis of the four elements.

Neighbourhood concentration may be reached by III 1–7, 10; VI; and VII.

The first *jhāna* may be reached by II 1–10 and III 8.

The first three *jhānas* may be reached by IV 1–3.

The four *jhānas* may be reached by I 1–10 and III 9.

The fourth *jhāna* may be reached by IV 4.

The immaterial attainments may be reached by V 1–4.

The acquired image (*uggaha-nimitta*) and counter-image (*paṭibhāga-nimitta*) will arise only on realizing I 1–10; II 1–10; III 8, 9: hence in twenty-two exercises.

For a full explanation of these forty exercises, see Vism III–XI.

For further details about *jhāna,* etc., see Fund. IV.

§76 Ten Kasiṇas

The *kasiṇa* (possibly related to Skt *kṛtsna* = complete, total, hence "completion" or "totalization") forms a purely external method of inducing concentration and reaching the *jhānas.* Superficially it resembles somewhat certain methods of inducing hypnotic sleep, etc., by gazing at bright objects. In order, therefore, to avoid such an outcome, one should beware of sleepiness and strive to keep the mind fully alert. One begins with concentrating one's undivided attention on one of the objects given above. In the colour *kasiṇas*, a blue, yellow, red or white disk made of cloth, flowers, and the like may serve as preliminary object. In the earth *kasiṇa,* the object of gazing may be a ploughed field seen from afar, or a round piece of earth prepared for the purpose. In the water *kasiṇa* one may gaze at a pond seen from a higher elevation, or at water contained in a vessel. Similarly with the fire and wind *kasiṇas.*

At first one should fix the whole attention on the disk, say a blue disk, as the preliminary object and so produce the so-called preliminary concentration (*parikamma-samādhi*). Now, while constantly gazing at the disk, one must strive to remain mentally alert and awake in order not to fall into a hypnotic sleep, as already pointed out. At the same time one must keep from the mind all outside impressions and thoughts on other objects, as well as all those disturbing and often dangerous mental visions that may arise.

Now, while exclusively fixing the eyes and thoughts on the blue disk as the sole object, the things around the disk seem to disappear and the disk itself seems to become more and more a mere mental phantom. Then, whether the eyes are opened or closed, one perceives the mentalized *kasiṇa* disk, which more and more assumes the appearance of the bright orb of the moon. This is the so-called acquired image (*uggaha-nimitta*) which, though apparently seen by means of the physical eyes, is nevertheless produced and seen only by the mind independent of the sense activity of the eye.

As soon as this mentally produced image becomes steady and no longer vanishes, but remains steadily fixed in the mind, one should, according to Vism IV,30 move to another place and there continue the exercise. In fixing more and more the mental eye on the mentally produced image or light, it becomes continually steadier and brighter, till at last it may assume the appearance of the bright morning star or something similar. At this point the mental counter-image (*paṭibhāga-nimitta*) is attained, and along with it the so-called neighbourhood concentration (*upacāra-samādhi*).

Already during this stage all mental hindrances (*nīvaraṇa*) have, at least temporarily, disappeared and arise no more. No sensual lust (*kāmacchanda*) arises in such a state. No ill-will (*vyāpāda*) can irritate the mind. All mental stiffness and dullness (*thīna-middha*) are overcome. No restlessness and anxiety (*uddhacca-kukkucca*) and no wavering doubt and scepticism (*vicikicchā*) can any more divert the mind. As long as it is possible for these five mental hindrances to arise, there can be no lasting tranquillity of the mind. Now, by tenaciously fixing the mind on the counter-image, one eventually reaches the "attainment concentration" (*appanā-samādhi*) and thereby enters into the first *jhāna*. And by becoming more and more absorbed, and by the gradual vanishing, one by one, of abstract thought and discursive thinking, of rapture and joy, one consecutively passes through the remaining *jhānas*.

By the *jhānas* are meant supersensual states of perfect mental absorption in which the fivefold sense activity has ceased, and which can only be attained in absolute solitude and by unremitting perseverance in the development of concentration. No visual or audible impressions arise at such a time, only bodily feeling is left. In this state the monk appears to the outside world as if dead. But, although all the sense impressions such as seeing, hearing, etc., have disappeared, still the mind remains active, perfectly alert and fully awake.

1. The first *jhāna* is a state of peace, ecstasy, and joyful bliss, yet thought conception and discursive thinking (*vitakka-vicāra*), i.e. the so-called "inner speech," or "verbal activities of the mind" (*vacī-saṅkhāra*), are still at work.
2. As soon as these verbal activities of the mind have ceased, one has attained the second *jhāna*, which is a state of highest rapture and happiness (*pīti-sukha*), free from thinking and pondering.
3. After the fading away of rapture, the third *jhāna* is reached, marked by equanimous happiness (*upekkhā-sukha*).
4. After the complete fading away of happiness, a state of perfect equanimity (*upekkhā*) reigns, called the fourth *jhāna*.

After emerging from the fourth *jhāna*, the mind becomes "serene, pure, lucid, stainless, devoid of evil, pliable, able to act, firm and imperturbable" (see Fund. IV). For a detailed explanation of the *kasiṇa* exercises see Vism IV, V.

§77 AN 10:29

There are ten *kasiṇa* spheres, O monks. And which are these?

Herein someone perceives earth as his *kasiṇa*, above, below, round about, undivided, without bounds.

Again, someone perceives water as his *kasiṇa* ... fire ... wind ... blue ... yellow ... red ... white ... space ... consciousness, above, below, round about, undivided, without bounds.

These are the ten *kasiṇa* spheres, O monks. It is considered as the highest of these *kasiṇa* spheres, however, for someone to perceive consciousness as his *kasiṇa*, above, below, round about, undivided, without bounds.

There are beings with such perception, O monks. But also regarding the beings with such perception, there may be noticed impermanence and change. Understanding thus, O monks, the wise noble disciple turns away from it. And turning away from it he becomes detached from the highest, how much more so from lower things.

§78 Eight Stages of Mastery (*abhibhāyatana*)

DN 33

1. Perceiving forms on one's own body, one sees external forms, small ones, beautiful or ugly ones; and mastering these, one understands: "I know, I understand." This is the first stage of mastery.
2. Perceiving forms on one's own body, one sees forms externally, large ones.... This is the second stage of mastery.
3. Not perceiving forms on one's own body, one sees forms externally, small ones.... This is the third stage of mastery.
4. Not perceiving forms on one's own body, one sees forms externally, large ones.... This is the fourth stage of mastery.
5. Not perceiving forms on one's own body, one sees forms externally, blue forms, forms of blue hue, blue appearance, blue lustre; and mastering these, one understands: "I know, I understand." This is the fifth stage of mastery.

(6–8) The same is repeated with yellow, red, and white forms.

(1–2) As a preparatory *kasiṇa* object of the first and second exercises one should choose on one's own body a small or a big spot, beautiful or ugly, and thereon one should concentrate one's full undivided attention so that this object, after a while, reappears as a mental reflex or image (*nimitta*) and, as it were, as something external.

(3–4) In the third and fourth exercises the monk gains through an external *kasiṇa* object the mental images and the *jhānas*.

(5–8) As objects for the last four exercises, bright colours, flowers, clothes, etc., may be chosen.

A small *kasiṇa* object is considered suitable for a mentally unsteady nature (*vitakka-carita*), a large one for a dull nature (*moha-carita*), a beautiful one for an angry nature (*dosa-carita*), an ugly one for a lustful nature (*rāga-carita*).

§79 **Perception of Light** (*āloka-saññā*)

DN 33

Which concentration, O brothers, developed and often practised, may lead to the attainment of the eye of wisdom?

Herein the monk contemplates the perception of light, fixes his mind on the perception of day, and as at daytime so at night, and as at night so in the day. In this way, with wakeful and stainless mind, he develops a state of consciousness accompanied by light. This concentration, developed and often practised, leads to the attainment of the eye of wisdom.

Vism XIII, 95 says that this state of mind is a condition for reaching the knowledge of the divine eye (*dibba-cakkhu*). In other places it is said that this exercise dispels torpor and languor.

§80 **ten cemetery meditations**
(Meditation on Loathsomeness)
(*asubha-bhāvanā*)

DN 22; MN 10

Just as if, O monks, the monk should see a corpse thrown to the burial ground, one, two, or three days dead, swollen up, blue-black in colour, full of corruption; he draws the conclusion as to his own body: "This my body too has this nature, has this destiny, cannot escape it."

And further, just as if the monk should see a corpse thrown to the burial ground, eaten by crows, hawks, or vultures, by dogs or jackals, or gnawed by all kinds of worms; he draws the conclusion as to his own body: "This my body too has this nature, has this destiny, cannot escape it."

And further, just as if the monk should see a framework of bones, flesh hanging from it, bespattered with blood, held together by the sinews....

A framework of bones, stripped of flesh, bespattered with blood, held together by the sinews....

A framework of bones, without flesh and blood, but still held together by the sinews....

Bones disconnected and scattered in all directions, here a bone of the hand, there a bone of the foot; here a shin bone; there a thighbone; here the pelvis, there the spine, there the skull....

Bones, bleached and resembling shells....

Bones, heaped together after the lapse of years....

Bones, weathered and crumbled to dust; he draws the conclusion as to his own body: "This my body too has this nature, has this destiny, cannot escape it."

AN 4:14

There, O monks, the monk keeps firmly in his mind a favourable object that has arisen, such as the mental image of a skeleton, or a corpse infested by worms, or a corpse blue-black in colour, or a festering corpse, or a corpse riddled with holes, or a corpse swollen up.

§81 The Ten Contemplations (*anussati*)

AN 1:16.1–10

There is one contemplation, O monks, which, developed and frequently practised, leads to the complete turning away from the world, to detachment, cessation, peace, penetrating knowledge, enlightenment, and Nibbāna. And which is that one contemplation?

The contemplation of the Enlightened One ... the Dhamma ... the Community of noble disciples ... morality ... liberality. ... the heavenly beings ... death ... the body ... in-and-out breathing ... peace. This is one contemplation, O monks, which, developed and frequently practised, leads to the complete turning away from the world, to detachment, cessation, peace, penetrating knowledge, enlightenment, and Nibbāna.

According to the commentary, the contemplation of the Enlightened One may serve two purposes: (1) as "means to inner stimulation," (2) as object of developing insight (*vipassanā*).

(1) Whenever, for example, one with the intention of gaining the first *jhāna* carries out one of the suitable exercises, let us say, a cemetery meditation, but his mind is unsteady and wanders unsatisfied to and fro—just as an untamed bull runs hither and thither—then he should at first avoid this exercise and reflect upon the mundane and supramundane qualities of the Enlightened One. Hereby his mind is cheered and becomes gradually free from the five mental hindrances to the attaining of right concentration (i.e. lust, anger, torpor and languor, restlessness and worry, sceptical doubt). After his mind has thus become calm, the initial exercise (cemetery contemplation) may lead him to the desired goal. Just as a man who finds it impossible with a blunt axe to cut a tree first gets his axe sharpened in order to accomplish his purpose, just so the monk at first tames and subdues his mind by means of the contemplation of the Buddha in order to become able to carry out his initial exercise with success.

(2) As object or starting point of the development of insight (*vipassanā*), the contemplation of the Buddha serves in the following way: Whoever, after rising from the concentration reached by the contemplation of the Buddha, ponders over the real nature of the "contemplator," comes to understand that only the conscious state associated with the contemplation had been present (but no ego-entity, or self). And he knows that this state represents the consciousness group; the feeling associated therewith, the feeling group; the perception associated therewith, the perception group; the mental formations simultaneously arising therewith, the mental-formations group (volition, impression, advertence, etc.). And he further knows

that these four mental groups cannot arise without the physical base of mind, that this physical base again is a name for the four primary elements (solid, fluid, heat, motion), and that again all these things form the corporeality group.

Now, in contemplating the five groups of existence, the monk understands these five groups as suffering, understands the rebirth-producing craving as the cause of suffering, understands the cessation of craving as the cessation of suffering, understands the Noble Eightfold Path as the path leading to the cessation of suffering. By means of this insight he comes, step by step, nearer and nearer to the attainment of arahatship. In this way the contemplation of the Buddha has served as object and starting point for the development of insight.

AN 6:10

Once the Blessed One dwelt in the Figtree Grove near Kapilavatthu, in the country of the Sakyas. And the Sakya Mahānāma went to the Blessed One, saluted him reverentially, sat down on one side, and said:

"Venerable One, when a noble disciple has made progress and understood the teaching, in which state does such a one frequently dwell?"

Such a one, Mahānāma, dwells frequently in the following state:

(1) Contemplation of the Buddha

Herein, Mahānāma, the noble disciple contemplates the Perfect One: "Truly he, the Blessed One, is holy, a fully enlightened one, perfect in knowledge and conduct, sublime, a knower of the worlds, the incomparable leader of persons to be tamed, the master of humans and gods, enlightened, blessed."

(2) Contemplation of the Doctrine

Further, Mahānāma, the noble disciple contemplates the Dhamma (Doctrine): "Well proclaimed is the Dhamma by the Blessed One, visible in this life, of immediate result, inviting, leading onward, comprehensible by the wise, each for himself.'"

(3) Contemplation of the Community

Further, Mahānāma, the noble disciple contemplates the Community of noble disciples: "Of noble conduct is the Community of noble disciples of the Blessed One, of upright conduct, of right conduct, of dutiful conduct; namely, the four pairs of noble disciples or the eight individuals.[1] This Community of the disciples of the Blessed One is worthy of sacrifices, worthy of hospitality, worthy of gifts, worthy of reverential salutation, an incomparable field for merit in the world."

(4) Contemplation of Morality

Further, Mahānāma, the noble disciple contemplates his own morals which are unbroken, without rent, immaculate, undefiled, liberating, praised by the wise, and leading to concentration.

(5) Contemplation of Liberality

Further, Mahānāma, the noble disciple contemplates his own liberality: "Truly, blessed am I, highly blessed: that among creatures soiled with the defilement of meanness, I am living with a heart free from niggardliness, accessible to beggars, pleased by giving and sharing with others."

(6) Contemplation of Heavenly Beings

Further, Mahānāma, the noble disciple contemplates the heavenly beings: "There are the heavenly beings of the retinue of the Four Great Kings, the heavenly beings of the World of the Thirty-three, of the Yāma World, the Blissful Beings, those rejoicing in their own creations, those with power over the creations of others, those of the Brahma world, and those still above them. Now, such faith, morality,

1 These are the attainers of the paths and fruits of stream-entry, once-returning, non-returning, and arahatship. (See B. Dict.: ariya-puggala.)

knowledge, liberality, and wisdom, endowed with which these beings, after leaving this world, have reappeared there, such qualities as these are also to be found in me."

When, indeed, the noble disciple contemplates thus, at such a time his heart is neither ensnared by greed, nor by hatred, nor by delusion. Uplifted is his mind at such a time, based on contemplation. And with uplifted mind, Mahānāma, the noble disciple gains understanding of the Dhamma, delight in the Dhamma. Being delighted, there arises rapture in him. Being filled with rapture in his heart, inwardly he becomes calmed. And being inwardly calmed he feels happiness; and the mind of the happy one becomes collected.

Of this noble disciple, Mahānāma, it is said that among misguided humankind he walks on the right path, that among suffering humankind he lives free from suffering. And as one who has entered the stream of the Dhamma, he develops his contemplation.

When, Mahānāma, a noble disciple has reached the fruit and understood the doctrine, such a one frequently dwells in this state.

> The first three of these contemplations are the meditations most favoured in all Southern Buddhist countries. They are recited by old and young, e.g. when offering flowers before the Buddha image.

§82

(7) Contemplation of Death
(maraṇānusati)

In Vism VIII,4 it is said: One who wishes to develop this exercise should go into solitude, and while in seclusion he should consider deeply: "Death will come; the life faculty will come to an end": or: "I am destined to die! I am destined to die!" To him, in fact, who does not undertake this consideration in the right way, there may arise grief, when thinking for example about the death of a beloved person, just as in the case of a mother when thinking on the death of her child. And when considering the death of a person regarded with dislike, joy may spring up, just as in the case of enemies thinking on the death of their enemies; yet, when thinking on the death of a person regarded with indifference, no emotion will be aroused, just as in the case of a cremator of dead bodies while looking at a dead body. While thinking on one's own death, however, horror may arise, just as in one who sees a murderer with drawn sword standing before him. But when seeing here and there bodies of the slain or other dead beings, one may reflect on the death of such beings who once had lived in happiness, and one may incite one's mindfulness, emotions, and wisdom and consider thus: "Death will come." Only in one who practises the contemplation on death in this way will mindfulness become firmly established, and the mental exercise will reach neighbourhood concentration (*upacāra-samādhi*).

According to Vism VIII,8, one may also contemplate on death in the following way: One may consider death like a murderer with a drawn sword standing in front of one; or one may consider that all happiness ends in death; or that even the mightiest beings in the world cannot escape death; or that this body must be shared by us with innumerable worms and other beings living in it; or that life is something depending on in-and-out breathing; or that life functions only as long as the elements, food, and breath are functioning properly; or that nobody knows when, where, and through what one will die; or what kind of destiny awaits us after death; or that life is very short and limited.

§83 **AN 8:74**

Contemplation on death, O monks, developed and frequently practised, brings high reward and blessing, has the Deathless as goal and end. And how so?

As soon, O monks, as the day draws to a close, or when the night vanishes and the day breaks, the monk thinks to himself: "Truly, there are many possibilities of dying: a serpent may bite me, or a scorpion or centipede may sting me, and thereby I may lose my life. But this would be for me an obstruction. Or I may stumble and fall down; or the food taken by me may disagree with me. Bile, phlegm, or pricking gases may become stirred up. Men or evil spirits may attack me, and thereby I may lose my life. But that would be for me an obstruction." Here, the monk has to consider: "Are there still found in me unsubdued evil and unwholesome states which, if I should die today or tonight, would lead me to misfortune (in the next life)?"

Now, if the monk in his reflections notices that there are still unsubdued evil and unwholesome states found in him, then he should use his utmost determination, energy, exertion, perseverance, steadfastness, mindfulness, and clear comprehension in order to subdue these evil and unwholesome states.

If, however, the monk in his reflections notices that there are no more found in him any evil and unwholesome states which, if he should die, would lead him to misfortune, then this monk should dwell in blissful joy, training himself in all good things by day and by night.

§84 **AN 7:46**

If, O monks, a monk often entertains the thought of death, his mind will shrink from attachment to life, will turn away from it, get detached from it, will not feel drawn to it, and equanimity or disgust will make their appearance.

Just as, O monks, a cock's feather or a piece of bowstring, thrown into the fire, shrinks, twists, rolls itself up, no more stretches itself out: just so the mind shrinks back from attachment to life, turns away from it, gets detached from it, does not feel drawn to it, and equanimity or disgust make their appearance.

If, however, the monk, though he often entertains the idea of death, still has attachment to life, and no disgust makes its appearance, then the monk should know that he has not developed the idea of death, and that he has not reached successive stages of distinction, and that he has not reached the full strength of that meditation. In this way he has a clear comprehension of it.

If, however, in a monk, who often entertains the idea of death, his mind shrinks from attachment to life, turns away from it, gets detached from it, does not feel drawn to it, and equanimity or disgust make their appearance, then this monk should know that he has developed the idea of death, and that he has reached successive stages of distinction, and that he has reached the full strength of that meditation. In this way he has a clear comprehension of it.

§85 **SN 4:10**

The days and nights are flying past,
Life dwindles hurriedly away:
The life of mortals vanishes
Like water in a tiny stream.

AN 7:70

Short, alas, is the life of man, limited and fleeting, full of pain and torment. One should wisely understand this, do good deeds, and lead a holy life; for no mortal ever escapes death.

Just as the dewdrop at the point of the grass blade at sunrise very soon vanishes and does not remain for long: just so is the life of humans like a dewdrop, very short and fleeting.

Or, just as at the pouring down of a mighty rain-cloud the bubbles on the water very soon vanish and do not remain for long: just so is the bubble-like life of humans very short and fleeting.

Or, just as a furrow drawn with a stick in the water very soon vanishes and does not remain for long: just so is the furrow-like life of humans very short and fleeting.

Or, just as a strong man forms a ball of spittle with the tip of his tongue and without any effort spits it out: just so is the life of humans like a ball of spittle, very short and fleeting.

Or, just as if one throws a lump of meat into a metal pot heated for a full day, the meat at once dissolves and does not remain for long: just so is the life of humans like a lump of meat, very short and fleeting.

Or, just as cattle for slaughter, whatever foot they lift, ever stand on the brink of death: just so is the life of humans like cattle for slaughter, very short and fleeting.

One should wisely understand this, do good deeds, and lead a holy life; for no mortal ever escapes death.

§86 **Snp 576**

As in the morning one may fear
The falling of the ripened fruits,
So all mortals in this world
Live in constant fear of death.

SN 3:22

All beings are subject to death, end in death, can never escape death.

As every earthen pot that has
Been fashioned by the potter's hand,
No matter whether small or great,
Will fall to pieces in the end:

Just so are all beings subject to death, end in death, can never escape death.

All beings some time have to die,
Their life one day will end in death,
And they will fare after their deeds,
And good or bad fruits they will earn.

The evil-doer fares to hell,
The good man to a happy world.
Hence, noble deeds you should perform
As a provision for the next life,
For good deeds in the next world give
To living beings a strong support.

§87 SN 35:36

All things, O monks, are subject to death. And which are these?

The eye is subject to death, visible forms are subject to death, visual consciousness is subject to death, visual impression is subject to death, and also feeling conditioned through visual impressions—agreeable, disagreeable, and indifferent feeling—this too is subject to death.

The ear, sounds, and auditory consciousness.... The nose, odours, and olfactory consciousness.... The tongue, taste, and gustatory consciousness.... The body, bodily impressions, and body-consciousness.... The mind, mind-objects, and mind-consciousness, mental impression, and also the feeling conditioned through mental impression—agreeable, disagreeable, and indifferent—feeling, this too is subject to death.

Comprehending thus, the noble disciple turns away from the eye, visible forms, visual consciousness; from the ear ... nose ... tongue ... body ... mind, mind-objects, mind-consciousness, mental impression, and the feeling conditioned through mental impression. Turning away from these, he becomes detached; through detachment he becomes liberated; and in the Liberated One the knowledge arises: "Liberated am I"; and he understands: "Rebirth has ceased, the holy life is fulfilled, the task is done, and nothing further remains after this."

§88 SN 3:25

Just as the mighty rocky mounts
Are stretching high up to the sky,
Traversing all the land around,
And weighing heavily on it;

Just so old age and death suppress
All living beings in this world,
The warriors, brahmans, traders, slaves,
The sweepers and the outcasts, too,
Not sparing anything whatever,
And crushing all that they can find.

Dhp 41

Alas, this mortal body soon
Will lie prostrate upon the ground,

Cast off, a thing lifeless and dead,
Just like a useless wooden log.

Dhp 46

If you have understood this body as foam,
Have known it as illusion, as mirage,
Then Māra's flower-arrows you will break,
And by the Lord of Death no more be found.

Dhp 47

Whose mind, like one who gathers flowers,
Does firmly cling to lovely things,
Him death will surely carry off,
Just as the flood the sleeping town.

§89 Here may be added a significant passage from Vism VIII,1: "In the ultimate sense, beings have only a very short moment to live, only as long as one single moment of consciousness lasts. Just as the cart wheel, in rolling forward as in standing still, every time rests merely on one point of its circumference: just so the life of a being lasts only as long as one single moment of consciousness lasts. As soon as this moment is extinguished, the being is considered as extinguished. For it is said:

All life and all existence here,
With all its joy and all its pain,
Depends all on one state of mind,
And quick that moment passes by.

§90 **(8) Contemplation of the Body**

(kāyagatāsati)

In the Suttas, e.g. MN 119, this contemplation refers frequently to all those concentration exercises mentioned as *kāyānupassanā*, or first *satipaṭṭhāna* (§129), some of which are also, at the same time, used as insight exercises. Here, however, within the forty concentration exercises, and in conformity with Vism VIII I, 2 it refers only to one of these contemplations, that on the thirty-two parts of the body. It is well known and frequently practised in all the Buddhist countries of Southern Asia.

MN 10; DN 22

Herein, O monks, the monk contemplates this body from the soles of the feet upward, and from the top of the hair downward, with a skin stretched over it, and filled with many impurities: "This body consists of (1–5) hairs of the head, hairs of the body, nails, teeth, skin; (6–10) flesh, sinews, bones, marrow, kidneys; (11–15) heart, liver, diaphragm, spleen, lungs; (16–20) intestines, mesentery, stomach, excrement, and brain;[2] (21–26) bile, phlegm, pus, blood, sweat, fat; (27–32) tears, skin-grease, spittle, nasal mucus, oil of the joints, and urine."

Just as if there were a sack, with openings at both sides, filled with various kinds of grain, with different kinds of paddy, beans, sesamum, and husked rice, and a man not blind opened it and examined its contents thus: "That is paddy, these are beans, this is sesamum, this is husked rice": just so does the monk investigate this body.

§91 According to Vism VIII,49, one who wishes to develop this contemplation should at first learn by heart the names of the thirty-two parts of the body, recite them again and again, and thereafter repeat them mentally. This should be done in groups. At first the fivefold group ending with skin (i.e. 1–5) should be learned by heart, forward and backward, and then recited; thereafter the fivefold kidney-group (6–10), then the fivefold lung-group (11–15), then the fivefold brain-group (16–20), then the sixfold fat-group (21–26), then the sixfold urine-group (27–32). Hence: (1–5) hair of the head, hair of the body, nails, teeth, skin; (5–1) skin, teeth, nails, hair of the body, hair of the head; (6–10) flesh, sinews, bones, marrow, kidneys; (10–6) kidneys, marrow, bones, sinews, flesh, etc.

2 To the thirty-one parts of the body mentioned in the Suttas (e.g. MN 10 and DN 22) "brain" is added in the commentaries.

He should determine each single part of the body with regard to colour, shape, bodily region (upper or lower), place, and its boundaries; and he should not proceed too quickly during the contemplation of the single part. In the Suttas this contemplation is generally used as a concentration exercise, sometimes however as an insight exercise, for example, when used as an analysis of the four elements (see §128).

The first *jhāna* may arise during the contemplation of any of the thirty-two parts of the body. In Vism VIII,140 it is further said: "If now, while all the parts of the body appear distinctly, one directs one's attention outwardly, all men and animals lose the appearance of living beings and seem to be heaps of manifold bodily parts. And it looks as if the foods and drinks swallowed by them were being inserted into these heaps of bodily things." Now, while again and again considering the idea: "How disgusting! How disgusting!", and leaving out several parts, one after the other, there will arise after a while full concentration (*appanā-samādhi*), i.e. the first *jhāna*.

In this exercise the visualizing of colour, shape, region, place, or boundaries counts as acquired image (*uggaha-nimitta*); the visualizing of the loathsomeness of all the bodily parts, however, counts as counter-image (*paṭibhāga-nimitta*). Now, while practising and developing the counter-image, there may arise full concentration in the form of the first *jhāna*.

§92 **(9) Mindfulness of In-and-Out Breathing** (*ānāpānasati*)

This is one of the most important exercises, even the most important of all, especially if considered under the sixteen different ways of carrying it out. As a concentration exercise it may bring about all four *jhānas*. In MN 118 it is treated as an exercise both for concentration and insight.

SN 54:9

The concentration achieved by mindfulness of in-and-out breathing, O monks, developed and frequently practised, is peaceful and sublime, an undefiled and blissful state, which dispels at once the recurring evil and unwholesome states and brings them to a standstill. Just as in the last month of the hot season a suddenly arising mighty rain will make the whirled-up dirt and dust at once disappear and bring them to a standstill, just so the concentration of mindfulness on in-and-out breathing, developed and frequently practised, makes the repeatedly arising evil and unwholesome states disappear at once and brings them to a standstill. And how so?

There the monk retires to the forest, to the foot of a tree, or to a solitary place, seats himself cross-legged, body erect, his mindfulness fixed before him. Mindfully he breathes in, mindfully he breathes out.

I. (1) Making a long inhalation, he knows: "I make a long inhalation"; making a long exhalation, he knows: "I make a long exhalation."

(2) Making a short inhalation, he knows: "I make a short inhalation"; making a short exhalation, he knows: "I make a short exhalation."

(3) "Clearly perceiving the entire (breath-) body, I shall breathe in": thus he trains himself; "clearly perceiving the entire (breath-) body, I shall breathe out": thus he trains himself.

(4) "Calming this bodily function, I shall breathe in": thus he trains himself; "calming this bodily function, I shall breathe out": thus he trains himself.

II. (5) "Feeling rapture, I shall breathe in": thus he trains himself; "feeling rapture, I shall breathe out": thus he trains himself.

(6) "Feeling joy, I shall breathe in": thus he trains himself; "feeling joy, I shall breathe out": thus he trains himself.

(7) "Feeling the mental formation, I shall breathe in": thus he trains himself; "feeling the mental formation, I

shall breathe out": thus he trains himself.

(8) "Calming the mental formation, I shall breathe in": thus he trains himself; "calming the mental formation, I shall breathe out": thus he trains himself.

III. (9) "Clearly perceiving the mind, I shall breathe in": thus he trains himself; "clearly perceiving the mind, I shall breathe out": thus he trains himself.

(10) "Cheering the mind, I shall breathe in": thus he trains himself; "cheering the mind, I shall breathe out": thus he trains himself.

(11) "Concentrating the mind, I shall breathe in": thus he trains himself; "concentrating the mind, I shall breathe out": thus he trains himself.

(12) "Freeing the mind, I shall breathe in": thus he trains himself; "freeing the mind, I shall breathe out": thus he trains himself.

IV. (13) "Contemplating impermanence, I shall breathe in": thus he trains himself; "contemplating impermanence, I shall breathe out": thus he trains himself.

(14) "Contemplating detachment, I shall breathe in": thus he trains himself; "contemplating detachment, I shall breathe out": thus he trains himself.

(15) "Contemplating cessation, I shall breathe in": thus he trains himself; "contemplating cessation, I shall breathe out": thus he trains himself.

(16) "Contemplating abandonment, I shall breathe in": thus he trains himself; "contemplating abandonment, I shall breathe out" thus he trains himself.

Thus, O monks, developed and frequently practised, the concentration of mindfulness on in-and-out breathing is peaceful and sublime, an undefiled and blissful state, which makes the repeatedly arising evil and unwholesome states disappear at once and brings them to a standstill.

§93 I (1–2) In practising mindfulness of breathing, attention should be directed to a place somewhere between the upper lip and the tip of the nose, and should never follow the course of respiration, as in that case the mind will become distracted. It is best that the eyes be either closed or slightly open. The breathing can be noticed by the bodily impact, warmth, coolness, etc., or by the slight noise produced by the passage of the air, or by the odour accompanying the in-breathing.

In the monk who, with right mindfulness, develops this exercise, the restraint present therein counts as the training in higher morality (*adhisīla-sikkhā*), the concentration present therein as the training in higher mentality (*adhicitta-sikkhā*), the knowledge present therein as the training in higher wisdom (*adhipaññā-sikkhā*).

In order to facilitate his concentration on the in-and-out breathing, the beginner may at first mentally count his respirations, but only up to ten, and then begin over and over again, namely: "one, one; two, two; three, three" etc., up to ten. There are still other effective expedients taught by the meditation teachers in Burma. All of them should only serve to prevent the arising of distracted thought not connected with the breathing. As soon, however, as the mind gets more and more concentrated and the mental image becomes steady, one should drop these auxiliary devices.

In some persons already after a very short time the two mental images may appear. Thereafter, through continued attention to the counter-image, and increasing the mental concentration more and more, one may finally reach the *jhānas*.

Now, having gained one of the *jhānas*, the monk after some time rises again from this *jhāna* and contemplates the conditioned arising of all these physical and mental phenomena of existence and understands everything as impermanent, suffering, and non-self. And in consequence of his deep insight into the continual dissolution and vanishing of all forms of existence, he turns away from them, becomes detached, and gains, one after the other, the four supramundane paths, and finally arahatship or full deliverance.

I (3–4) Now, while the training monk intentionally makes ever finer respirations, joy arises in him. By reason of this joy, he makes still finer respirations, till at last his mind turns away from them and equanimity arises.

II (5) "Feeling rapture," etc. means: "Making rapture clearly perceivable and distinct, I shall breathe in," etc. (Pṭs I, 186). Rapture is perceived as concentration object on entering the rapture-accompanied first two *jhānas*, as insight object during the subsequent contemplation of the impermanence and disappearance of the rapture experienced in the first two *jhānas*.

(7) "Mental formation" (*citta-saṅkhāra*) refers here to feeling and perception, as it is said (MN 44): "Perception and feeling are mental things: these things being bound up with mind, are mental formations."

III (10) "Cheering the mind" means: gladdening the mind, etc. This joy is gained by the meditating monk on entering the first three *jhānas* which are accompanied by happiness, and during the subsequent insight exercise when contemplating the impermanence and disappearance of the happiness experienced in the *jhānas*.

(12) "Freeing the mind" means freeing the mind through the first *jhāna* from the five hindrances (sensual lust, anger, etc.); through the second *jhāna* from thought conception and discursive thinking; through the third *jhāna* from rapture; through the fourth *jhāna* from agreeable and disagreeable feeling. Or, after rising from those *jhānas*, the training monk considers by way of insight the disappearance and impermanence, etc., of that state of consciousness that had been present during the *jhānas*. And thus through contemplating impermanence (*anicca*), he makes his mind free from the eternity-illusion; through contemplating suffering (dukkha), free from the happiness-illusion; through contemplating non-self (anattā), free from the self-illusion; through contemplating turning away, he makes it free from delight; through contemplating detachment, free from craving; through contemplating cessation, free from

the condition of arising (again); through contemplating abandoning, free from holding fast.

IV (13) "Impermanence" refers to the five groups of existence, namely, the corporeality group, the feeling group, etc.

(14–15) "Detachment" (*virāga*) and "cessation" (*nirodha*) refer to the dissolution of the five groups, and to Nibbāna.

(16) "Abandonment" (*paṭinissagga*) may mean two different things: (i) insight, as it represses, by way of "overcoming through its opposite," every wrong view, etc.; (ii) the supramundane path (of the stream-winner, etc.), as thereby the unwholesome qualities are forever abandoned. Thus, Group IV (13–16) is taught only with regard to pure insight, while Groups I–III are taught with regard to both mental tranquillity (*samatha*) and insight (*vipassanā*).

Stated briefly:

I. refers to the first *satipaṭṭhāna*, i.e. corporeality;
II. refers to the second, feeling;
III. refers to the third, consciousness or mind;
IV. refers to the fourth, mind-objects, including perception and mental formations.

About *satipaṭṭhāna,* see §129

§94 MN 118

Mindfulness of in-and-out breathing, O monks, developed and frequently practised, brings high reward and blessing. Mindfulness of in-and-out breathing, developed and frequently practised, brings the four applications of mindfulness to full perfection; these, perfect the seven factors of enlightenment; and these perfect wisdom and deliverance.

But how, O monks, does mindfulness of in-and-out breathing, developed and frequently practised, bring the four applications of mindfulness to full perfection?

I. Whenever the monk is mindful (1) in making a long inhalation or exhalation, or (2) in making a short inhalation or exhalation, or (3) is training himself to inhale or exhale while feeling the whole (breath-) body, or (4) is calming this bodily formation—at such a time the monk dwells in contemplation of the body, full of energy, clearly comprehending, mindful, subduing worldly greed and grief. Inhalation and exhalation, indeed, I call one among the bodily phenomena.

II. Whenever the monk trains himself to inhale and exhale while feeling (5) rapture (*pīti*), or (6) happiness (*sukha*), or (7) the mental formations (*citta-saṅkhāra*), or (8) while calming the mental formations—at such a time he dwells in contemplation of feeling, full of energy, clearly comprehending, mindful, after subduing worldly greed and grief. The full awareness of in-and-out breathing, indeed, I call one among the feelings.

III. Whenever the monk trains himself to inhale and exhale (9) while clearly perceiving the mind, or (10) while cheering the mind, or (11) while concentrating the mind, or (12) while setting the mind free—at such a time he dwells in contemplation of the mind, full of energy, clearly comprehending, mindful, after subduing worldly greed and grief. Without mindfulness and clear comprehension, indeed, there is no mindfulness of in-and-out breathing, I say.

IV. Whenever the monk trains himself to inhale and exhale while contemplating (13) impermanence, or (14) detachment, or (15) cessation, or (16) abandonment—at such a time he dwells in contemplation of the mind-objects, full of energy, clearly comprehending, mindful, after subduing worldly greed and grief. Having seen, through understanding, what is the abandoning of greed and grief, he looks on with perfect equanimity.

Mindfulness of in-and-out breathing, thus developed and frequently practiced, brings the four applications of mindfulness to full perfection.

§95 But how do the four applications of mindfulness, developed and frequently practised, bring the seven factors of enlightenment to full perfection?

1. Whenever the monk dwells in contemplation of body, feeling, mind, and mind-objects, full of energy, clearly comprehending, mindful, after subduing worldly greed and grief—at such a time his mindfulness is undisturbed; and whenever his mindfulness is present and undisturbed, at such a time he has gained and is developing the mindfulness factor of enlightenment (*sati-sambojjhaṅga*); and thus this factor of enlightenment reaches full perfection.

2. Whenever, while dwelling mindfully, he wisely investigates, examines, and considers the Dhamma, at such a time he has gained and is developing the investigation of the Dhamma factor of enlightenment (*dhamma-vicaya-sambojjhaṅga*); and thus this factor of enlightenment reaches full perfection.

3. Whenever, while wisely investigating, examining, and considering the Dhamma, his energy is firm and unshaken, at such a time he has gained and is developing the energy factor of enlightenment (*viriya-sambojjhaṅga*); and thus this factor of enlightenment reaches full perfection.

4. Whenever in him, while firm in energy, arises supersensuous rapture, at such a time he has gained and is developing the rapture factor of enlightenment (*pīti-sambojjhaṅga*); and thus this factor of enlightenment reaches full perfection.

5. Whenever, while enraptured in mind, his spiritual frame and his mind become tranquil, at such a time he has gained and is developing the tranquillity factor of enlightenment (*passaddhi-sambojjhaṅga*); and thus this factor of enlightenment reaches full perfection.

6. Whenever, while being tranquillized in his spiritual frame and happy, his mind becomes concentrated, at such a time he has gained and is developing the concentration factor of enlightenment (*samādhi-sambojjhaṅga*); and thus this factor of enlightenment reaches full perfection.

7. Whenever he looks on his mind with complete indifference, thus concentrated, at such a time he has gained and is developing the equanimity factor of

enlightenment (*upekkhā-sambojjhaṅga*); and thus this factor of enlightenment reaches full perfection.

The four applications of mindfulness thus developed and frequently practised, bring the seven factors of enlightenment to full perfection.

But how do the seven factors of enlightenment, developed and frequently practised, bring wisdom and deliverance (*vijjā-vimutti*) to full perfection?

Herein the monk develops the factors of enlightenment, bent on seclusion, detachment, and cessation, and leading to abandonment.

The seven factors of enlightenment, thus developed and frequently practised, bring wisdom and deliverance to full perfection.

§96 (10) Contemplation of Peace

By this contemplation is meant the contemplation of Nibbāna (see §§37–43). It therefore refers to the complete "cessation of all defilements" (*kilesa-parinibbāna*), as well as to the final "cessation of the groups of existence" (*khandha-parinibbāna*) attainable at the death of the arahat.

AN 1:16.10

One contemplation, O monks, developed and frequently practised, leads to the perfect turning away from the world, to detachment, cessation, peace, penetration, enlightenment, and Nibbāna. And which is this contemplation? It is the contemplation of peace.

AN 10:60

What, Ānanda, is the contemplation of cessation? There the monk goes to the forest, to the foot of a tree, or to an empty hut, and there he considers within himself thus: "This is peaceful, this is sublime, namely the coming to rest of all karma-formations, the abandoning of all substrata of existence, the vanishing of craving, cessation, Nibbāna. This, Ānanda, is called the contemplation of cessation.

AN 4:34

Whatever, O monks, there are of conditioned and unconditioned things, detachment is considered the highest of them, that is, the destruction of vanity, the overcoming of thirst, the rooting out of clinging, the breaking through the round of rebirths, the vanishing of craving, detachment, Nibbāna.

SN 43:12–44

The vanishing of greed, hate, and delusion: this, O monks is called the Unconditioned ... the Boundless ... Freedom from Bias ... the True ... the Further Shore ... the Subtle ... the Inconceivable ... the Ageless ... the Permanent ... the Beyond of all manifoldness ... the Peaceful ... the Deathless ... the Sublime ... the Auspicious ... the Safety ... the Wondrous ... the Sorrowless ... Nibbāna ... the Unoppressed ... the Detached ... the Isle ... the Shelter ... the Refuge ... the Final Aim.

AN 10:7

(Sāriputta:) "Once, brother Ānanda, I dwelt here near Sāvatthī in the Dark Wood. There I gained such a mental concentration that, though being in sight of earth, I was without perception of earth; though being in sight of water, I was without perception of water; though being in sight of fire, I was without perception of fire; though being in sight of wind, I was without perception of wind; though being in sight of the sphere of boundless space ... boundless consciousness, etc. ... though being in sight of this world, I was without perception of the world. But I still possessed perception."

"But which perception did the Venerable Sāriputta have on that occasion?"

"That Nibbāna consists in the cessation of (the process of) becoming (*bhava-nirodha*): this one perception arose in me, brother, and the other perception disappeared. Just as, brother, in a wood-fire one flame lights up, and the other flame disappears; just so there arose in me the perception that Nibbāna consists in the cessation of becoming, and the other perception disappeared. Thus this is the perception I had on that occasion: that Nibbāna consists in the cessation of becoming."

§97 The Four Divine Abodes (*brahma-vihāra*)

or

The Four Boundless States (*appamaññā*)

DN 33

There are four boundless states, O brethren:

Herein the monk with all-embracing kindness ... with compassion ...with altruistic joy ... with equanimity pervades first one direction, then the second, then the third, then the fourth, above, below, around, in every quarter. And identifying himself with all, he pervades the entire universe with all-embracing kindness, with compassion, with altruistic joy, with equanimity, with heart grown great, wide, deep, boundless, free from wrath and anger.

§98 I. Development of All-Embracing Kindness (*mettā-bhāvanā*)

Before taking up this exercise, the beginner should, according to Vism IX,2, first of all consider the evil consequences of hatred and the blessing of all-embracing kindness. For as long as one has not understood the evil consequences of a thing, so long one will not be able to overcome it. Similarly one cannot reach a noble state of mind before first understanding its blessing. As it is said:

AN 3:55

Because of hate, overwhelmed and fettered in mind by hate, one leads an evil life in bodily deeds, words, and thoughts, and understands according to reality neither one's own welfare, nor the welfare of others, nor the welfare of both. If, however, hatred is overcome, one leads no evil life, neither in bodily deeds, words, or thoughts, and one knows according to reality one's own welfare, the welfare of others, and the welfare of both.

§99 AN 11:16

If, O monks, the liberation of heart by all-embracing kindness has been cultivated and developed, made one's vehicle and foundation, is firmly established, brought to greatness and full perfection, one may expect eleven blessings: One sleeps peacefully; awakes peacefully; has no evil dreams; is dear to humans; is dear to spirits; heavenly beings protect one; fire, poison, and weapons cannot do any harm; the scattered mind becomes composed; one's features brighten up; one will have an untroubled death; and if one does not penetrate higher, one will be reborn in the Brahma-world.

In Vibh XIII,643 it is said: "But how does the monk whose mind is filled with all-embracing kindness pervade one direction? Just as, at the sight of a dear and agreeable person, one may feel kindness, just so does he pervade with his kindness all living beings."

§100 Pṭs II,130

In five ways the liberation of heart by all-embracing kindness is practised with unspecified extension: "May all beings be free from hate, oppression, and anxiety; may they pass their life in happiness! May all living beings ... all creatures ... all individuals ... all those included in personal existence be free from hate, oppression, and anxiety; may they pass their life in happiness!"

Snp 145

§101 "May all beings live in happiness and peace. And may their hearts be filled with joy and with delight!"

According to Vism IX,4–8, at the outset one should not direct one's kindness to a very dear person or to an indifferent person, also not to an enemy, or to a person of the other sex. First of all, one should begin with oneself: "Let me be happy, free from suffering!"

Or: "Let me be free from hate, oppression, and anxiety! Let me lead a life in happiness!"

Thereafter one should think: "Just as I love happiness and detest suffering, and as I wish to live and not to die, just so it is with other beings!"

§102 SN 3:8

Whatever quarter of the world I searched through, I found no one whom I loved better than myself. Just so to all others their self is most dear. Thus, wishing well to all, one should do harm to none.

At first, therefore, one should direct the all-embracing kindness to oneself, then to one's venerable teacher or a similar person, and think of his pure life, his insight, etc., and say to oneself: "Let this good and noble being be happy and free from suffering." Thereupon one should direct one's kindness to a dear friend, then to an indifferent person, then to an enemy.

If, however, resentment should arise when thinking of the enemy, then one should revert and concentrate one's kindness on the above-mentioned persons. However, should the monk, even after attaining the *jhāna*, still feel resentment against the enemy, then he should remember the simile of the saw, etc. (see next text).

§103 MN 21

If, O monks, robbers or highwaymen should use a double-handled saw to cut your limbs and joints, whoever gives way to anger would not be following my advice. For thus should you train yourselves: "Undisturbed shall our mind remain, no evil words shall escape our lips; friendly and full of sympathy shall we remain, with heart full of love, free from any hidden malice. And we shall penetrate those persons with loving thoughts, wide, deep, boundless, freed from anger and hatred."

§104 SN 7:2

Whoso repays hatred with hatred,
Is worse than he who hated first.
Who to the hater shows no hate
Is the one who wins the arduous fight.
A blessing will he be to both,
Himself and the other too,
Who, seeing others full of wrath,
Remains composed and clear in mind.

AN 7:60

The hater does not grasp the good,
Nor does he wish to see the truth,
For gloom and darkness reign supreme,
When hatred overpowers a man.
And if the hater puts the brake,
With difficulty or with ease,
If then his outburst comes to end,
He suffers from the fire within.

His looks his agitation show;
It's like the smoke of smould'ring fire.
From it again may hate-fire burst
And set ablaze the world of men.
He knows no shame, no moral dread,
Is lacking tact whenever he speaks,
And overpowered by his hate,
He nowhere any refuge finds.
Oneself is everyone's best friend,
Himself does everyone love most,
And yet in rage one kills oneself,
Made blind by various vanities.
Who others does deprive of life,
Who to his own life puts an end,
With hatred filled and overpowered,
Is unaware what he commits.

Thus, of this hate there may become
A deadly fetter quite concealed.

Break it to pieces, self-controlled,
With insight, wisdom, energy!

Just as the man who can see clear
Subdues his evil tendency,
So you should practise all good things
That no resentment may arise.

Redeemed from hate and from despair,
And rid of greed, from envy free,
The tamed ones have discarded hate
And reach Nibbāna, free from taint.

Should the meditator, in spite of all his exertions, not yet be able to subdue his grudge, then he should reflect on certain noble qualities of his enemy and take no notice of anything evil in him. But should he still not be able to master his grudge, then he should remember the words of the Buddha.

§105 AN 5:161

There are, O monks, five means of overcoming hatred, whereby the anger that has arisen in a monk may be overcome. And which are these?

To a person against whom hatred might arise, one should develop all-embracing kindness ... compassion ... equanimity ... or one should not pay him any attention ... or one should picture to oneself the law of the ownership of karma, i.e. that this person too is the owner and heir of his deeds, that he is sprung from them, that his deeds are his refuge, and that he will have his wholesome and unwholesome deeds as his inheritance. In this way the monk may overcome his hatred.

§106 The following verses, quoted at Vism IX,22, are apparently from the Sutta Piṭaka, source as yet untraced.

If in your domain the foe
Has hurt you, has offended you,
Why do you torture your own mind,
Which lies not in the foe's domain?
Your kin, kindly disposed to you,

You one time weeping left behind,
Why don't you leave your foe the hate
That brings you so much misery?
You're truly playing with this hate,
Which brings to ruin, with all its roots,
The moral life you wish to lead,
Can there exist a greater fool?

Because someone has done you harm,
You fly into a rage and wrath!
But why then, after all, will you
Yourself commit such evil deeds?

If somebody, to worry you,
Has done you some unpleasant thing,
Why do you worry then yourself
And thereby satisfy his wish?

If you in rage and wrath should do
To him some evil thing or not,
In any case you will torment
Yourself with pain that's born of hate.

If, out of rage and wrath, your foe
Should ever do you any harm,
Why do you imitate his deeds
And cherish hatred in your heart?

That wrath and hate through which the foe
Has done you some unpleasant thing,
That hate, indeed, you should destroy!
Why should you worry without cause?

As moment after moment all
Will vanish, so will vanish too
Those five groups that have done you harm.
Who is it then you're angry with?

If one man hates another man,
Whom does he hate if not himself!
You are the cause of your own pain,
Why do you hate the other man?

§107 Thus, the monk should ask himself against whom or what he actually feels hatred, whether against the corporeality group, the feeling group, the perception group, the mental formations group, or the consciousness group, as in the ultimate sense no self is to be found.

An almost infallible means to overcome ill-feeling towards the enemy is to present him with a gift or to exchange gifts with him. Still another means is to consider that the enemy in former births might have been a near relation of oneself. As it is said:

SN 15:14–19

Not easy is it, O monks, to find any being that, at some time in this long round of rebirths, has not been your mother or father, or brother or sister, or son or daughter.

§108 **The Hymn of Love**

Snp 143–52 and Khp IX

Whoever is intent on his own welfare
After he once has seen the tranquil realm,
He should be capable, upright, straight, and amenable,
Of gentle manners, without any pride;

Should be content and satisfied with little,
Not over-busy, moderate in living,
Calm in his senses, and endowed with wisdom,
Not being loud and greedy in the houses.

He should not commit the slightest wrong,
For which wise brothers may rebuke him.
May all live joyful and in safety,
And may their hearts be filled with happiness!

Whatever beings there exist,
Should they be weak, or strong, or otherwise,
All, whether long, short, thick, or thin,
Or great, small, or medium size,

Invisible or visible,
Those that live near and those that live afar,

Those that are born or search for birth,
May all be filled with happiness in heart!

No one should ever hurt another,
Despise another for whatever reason,
And never should in wrath and hatred
One wish another person pain.

Just as a mother her own child,
Her only son, protects with all her might,
Just so one may towards all that live
Develop one's mind in boundless kindness.

Thus toward all the world one should
Unfold one's mind with all-embracing kindness,
Above, below and round about,
Without depression, hate, and angry feeling.

Whether one stands, goes, sits, or lies,
As long as one is free from sloth and languor,
One may unfold this contemplation,
Which they call a divine abode.

Whoever, avoiding evil views,
Possesses virtue and clear understanding,
Has given up all sensuous greed,
Never enters any mother's womb again.

§109 It 27

This was uttered by the Blessed One, the Holy One. Thus have I heard:

Whatever, O monks, there are of worldly and meritorious things, all these are not worth one sixteenth of the liberation of the heart by all-embracing kindness. The liberation of the heart by all-embracing kindness radiates and shines, surpassing all.

As the light of all the stars is not one sixteenth of the moonlight, but the light of the moon, while radiating and shining, surpasses them all, just so whatever there are of worldly and meritorious things, all these are not worth one sixteenth of the liberation of the heart by all-embracing kindness. The liberation of the heart by all-embracing kindness radiates and shines, surpassing all.

As in autumn, in the last month of the rainy season, in a clear and cloudless sky the sun rises in the firmament and dispels the darkness of the whole universal space, just so whatever there are of worldly and meritorious things, all these are not worth one sixteenth of the liberation of the heart by all-embracing kindness. The liberation of the heart by all-embracing kindness radiates and shines, surpassing all.

§110 **2. Development of Compassion**
(*karuṇā-bhāvanā*)

According to Vibh XIII,653 one should at first direct one's compassion to some pitiable, deformed man, fallen into utter need and misery, distressed, poor and starving. As it is said:

> "But how does the monk with a mind filled with compassion pervade first one direction? Just as, when seeing one man living in misery and distress, one may feel compassion: just so the monk pervades all beings with compassion."
>
> Hence compassion, like all-embracing kindness, should at first not be directed to such a person as a very dear friend, etc. The blessings are the same as those of all-embracing kindness. Also the method of its development is the same.

§111 **3. Development of Altruistic Joy**
(*muditā-bhāvanā*)

This contemplation may at first be directed to a dear friend with overflowing joy, thinking: "How this being overflows with joy! How good! How pleasant!" In Vibh XIII,663 it is said:

> "And how does the monk with a mind filled with altruistic joy first pervade one direction? Just as, when seeing a kind and dear person, one feels joy, just so the monk pervades all beings with joy."

The blessings, as well as the method of development, etc., are the same as those of all-embracing kindness.

§112 **4. Development of Equanimity**

(*upekkhā-bhāvanā*)

This contemplation is at first to be directed to some perfectly indifferent person, as it is said in Vibh XIII,673:

> "And how does the monk with a mind filled with equanimity first pervade one direction? Just as, when seeing somebody who is neither agreeable nor disagreeable to oneself, one remains indifferent, just so the monk pervades all living beings with equanimity."

By this exercise all four *jhānas* may be attained. While the three former divine abodes lead only to the third *jhāna,* this exercise leads to the fourth *jhāna.*

SUPPLEMENTARY TEXTS

§113 AN 8:63

As soon, O monks, as your mind is steadfast, well fixed, and the evil unwholesome things do no more seize upon it, you should train yourselves thus: "I shall develop, frequently practise, take as vehicle and foundation, firmly establish, unfold, and bring to full perfection the liberation of the heart by all-embracing kindness ... compassion ... altruistic joy ... equanimity!" Thus, O monks, you should train yourselves!

As soon, however, as this concentration is developed and well practised, you should practise it with thought conception and discursive thinking (*vitakka, vicāra*: first *jhāna*); should practise it without thought conception and discursive thinking (second *jhāna*, etc.); should practise it with rapture; should practise it without rapture (third *jhāna*, etc.); should practise it with pleasure; should practise it with equanimity.

§114 DN 33

Once the liberation of the heart by all-embracing kindness has been developed and frequently practised, taken as vehicle and foundation, firmly established, unfolded, and brought to full perfection, it will be impossible, it cannot be, that ill-will may take possession of one's heart, for the liberation of the heart by all-embracing kindness is considered release from ill-will.

Once the liberation of the heart by compassion has been developed and frequently practised ... it will be impossible, it cannot be, that cruelty may take possession of one's heart, for the liberation of the heart by compassion is considered release from cruelty.

Once the liberation of the heart by altruistic joy has been developed and frequently practised ... it will be impossible, it cannot be, that displeasure may take possession of one's heart, for the liberation of the heart by altruistic joy is considered release from displeasure.

Once the liberation of the heart by equanimity has been developed and frequently practised ... it will be impossible, it cannot be, that greed may take possession of one's heart, for the liberation of the heart by equanimity is considered release from greed.

§115 SN 46:54

(1) How, O monks, does the liberation of the heart by all-embracing *kindness* reach development? What is its issue? Wherein does it culminate? What is its result, its end?

Herein the monk develops the factors of enlightenment accompanied by all-embracing kindness. Now, if with regard to something not disgusting he wishes to dwell in the perception of the disgusting, he dwells in the perception of the disgusting. If with regard to something disgusting he wishes to dwell in the perception of the non-disgusting, he dwells in the perception of the non-disgusting. If with regard to something partly disgusting, partly not disgusting, he wishes to dwell in the perception of the disgusting, he dwells in the perception of the disgusting. If he wishes to avoid both the disgusting and the non-disgusting, and to dwell in equanimity, attentive, clearly conscious, he dwells in equanimity, attentive, clearly conscious. Or he may attain deliverance through the *beautiful* (§130, No. 3). The liberation of the heart by all-embracing kindness culminates, indeed, in the beautiful, if here the wise monk does not penetrate to any higher deliverance.

(2) How, O monks, does the liberation of the heart by *compassion* reach development? What is its issue? Wherein does it culminate? What is its result, its end?

Herein the monk develops the factors of enlightenment accompanied by the liberation of the heart by compassion. Now, if with regard to something not disgusting he wishes to dwell in the perception of the disgusting, he dwells in the perception of the disgusting.... Or, through the total overcoming of perceptions of forms, and through the vanishing of the reflex perceptions and through non-attention to the perceptions of diversity, with the idea: "Unbounded is space," he reaches the sphere of *unbounded space* and abides therein. The liberation of the heart by compassion, indeed, culminates in the sphere of unbounded space, if here the wise monk does not penetrate to any higher deliverance.

(3) But how, O monks, does the liberation of the heart by *altruistic joy* reach development? What is its issue? Wherein does it culminate? What is its result, its end?

Herein the monk develops the factors of enlightenment accompanied by the liberation of the heart by altruistic joy. Now, if with regard to something not disgusting he wishes to dwell in the perception of the disgusting, he dwells in the perception of the disgusting.... Or, through the total overcoming of the sphere of unbounded space, and with the idea: "Unbounded is consciousness," he reaches the sphere of unbounded *consciousness* and abides therein. The liberation of the heart by altruistic joy, indeed, culminates in the sphere of unbounded consciousness, if here the wise monk does not penetrate to any higher deliverance.

(4) But how, O monks, does the liberation of the heart by *equanimity* reach development? What is its issue? Wherein does it culminate? What is its result, its end?

Herein the monk develops the factors of enlightenment accompanied by the liberation of the heart by equanimity.

Now, if with regard to something not disgusting he wishes to dwell in the perception of the disgusting, he dwells in the perception of the disgusting.... Or, through the total overcoming of the sphere of unbounded consciousness, and with the idea: "Nothing is there!" he reaches the sphere of nothingness and abides therein. The liberation of the heart by equanimity, indeed, culminates in the sphere of nothingness, if here the wise monk does not penetrate to any higher deliverance.

§116 The Ten Perfections

About the attainment of the Ten Perfections (*pāramī, pāramitā*; see B. Dict.) through the four divine abodes, Vism IX,124 says:

Once the monk has in this way understood the power of these four boundless states, culminating in the beautiful, etc., he also should know that these exercises will bring to perfection all the ten noble qualities, such as liberality, etc.

(1) The Great Beings (*mahāsatta = bodhisatta,* beings destined for Buddhahood) are intent on the welfare of all living beings, do not tolerate the suffering of beings and wish them long enjoyment of all their particular states of happiness; and, not inclining to any special side, they show them liberality (*dāna*) without considering whether they are worthy of gifts or not.

(2) By avoiding hurting living beings, they practise morality (*sīla*).

(3) In order to bring morality to perfection, they practise renunciation (*nekkhamma*).

(4) In order to attain clear understanding of what is wholesome and unwholesome for beings, they purify their wisdom (*paññā*).

(5) For the sake of their salvation and welfare, they continually exert their energy (*viriya*).

(6) Although through the highest energy they may have attained heroism, they are nevertheless full of forbearance (*khanti*).

(7) They will never break a promise to give or do something (truthfulness: *sacca*).

(8) With unshaken resolution (*adhiṭṭhāna*) they work for the safety and welfare of beings.

(9) With unshaken kindness (*mettā*) they serve them in a selfless manner.

(10) In their equanimity (*upekkhā*) they do not expect anything in return.

Thus, while bringing the Ten Perfections to their accomplishment, they at the same time realize all the noble qualities up to the ten powers (*dasa-bala*; see B. Dict.) the four kinds of self-confidence (see AN 4:8), the six kinds of spiritual powers (*abhiññā*: see B. Dict.), and the ten qualities of an Enlightened One."

Of the canonical scriptures only the two apocryphal works, Buddhavaṃsa and Cariyapiṭaka, enumerate the above Ten Perfections leading to Buddhahood.

§117 AN 1:20.2

Any monk who develops, even for a single moment, the liberation of the heart by all-embracing kindness .... the liberation of the heart by compassion ... the liberation of the heart by altruistic joy ... the liberation of the heart by equanimity, of such a monk it is said that he does not practise mental absorption in vain, that he follows the teaching and advice of the Master, that he does not unworthily eat the food offered by the people. But what should be said about those who practise these exercises perseveringly?

§118 AN 10:208

The noble disciple, O monks, freed from greed and grudge, undeluded, attentive and clearly conscious, with mind full of kindness ... compassion ... altrustic joy ... and equanimity, pervades first one direction, then a second one, then a third one, then the fourth one, just so above, below, around; and thus identifying himself with all, he pervades the whole world with mind wide, developed, unbounded, free from hate and ill-will. And he understands: "Formerly my mind was limited and undeveloped. Now, however, my mind is unlimited and developed, and no limited deed will there remain and persist."

What do you think, O monks: if a boy from his earliest childhood develops kindness, compassion, altruistic joy, or equanimity, will he then still do bad deeds?

"No, Venerable One."

But, if he no longer does bad deeds, will suffering then still attack him?

"Certainly not, Venerable One. How should anyone, without doing bad deeds, be still attacked by suffering!"

Kindness ... compassion ... altruistic joy ... equanimity should be developed, by men as well as by women. No man or woman, on departing this life, can retain this body. The mortal has mind as mediator. The monk, however, knows: "Whatever formerly I have done of bad deeds with this material body, all that I have still to atone for here, and nothing of it will follow me." So developed, the liberation of the heart by kindness, compassion, altruistic joy, and equanimity leads to never-return, unless the wise monk already during life penetrates to a higher deliverance.

§119

Four Immaterial Spheres
(*arūpāyatana*)

These four immaterial spheres, generally called the four immaterial *jhānas*, are subtle refinements of the fourth *jhāna* of the fine-material sphere, being characterized by the two factors of the fourth *jhāna*, namely: equanimity and concentration.

§120

(1) Sphere of Boundless Space
(*ākāsānañcāyatana*)

To attain this state one has at first, e.g. through one of the *kasiṇas*, to attain the fourth *jhāna*. Then one rises from the *jhāna* and considers the misery of all corporeal existence. And with the intention to reach the immaterial sphere, one extends the still present mental *kasiṇa* image up to boundless space, thinking "Space! Space! Endless is space!" and thus gets the *kasiṇa* image to disappear.

"Suppose, the opening of a provision basket, or of a large kettle, etc., is covered over with a cloth of a blue, yellow, red, white, or other colour, and a man comes and looks at it. After the cloth has been blown off by a gust, the man will still stand there and look at the empty space. Just so it is with space perception; for he who first was looking at the *kasiṇa* image with the *jhāna*-eye, will, as soon as that mental image has suddenly disappeared through the preparatory consideration: "Space!, Space!, Space!' thereafter remain looking at mere space" (Vism X,11). As it is said:

§121 DN 33

Through the total overcoming of perceptions of forms, through the vanishing of the reflex perceptions, and through non-attention to the perceptions of diversity, with the idea: "Unbounded is space," the monk reaches the sphere of unbounded space and abides therein.

At Vibh XII,602 it is said: "There are those who have reached the attainment of the fine-material sphere, or have been reborn therein, or are enjoying present happiness (of the *jhānas*). Thus, whatever there exists for them of perception, of perceiving, of the having perceived, these are called the 'perceptions of forms' (*rūpa-saññā*)."

"By 'reflex perceptions' (*paṭigha-saññā*) one has to understand those perceptions that have arisen through the reflex action of the sense organs, as eye, etc., on the visual and other objects" (Vism X,16). As it is said in Vibh XII,603:

"What are here the reflex perceptions? They are the perceptions of visual objects, sounds, odours, tastes, and bodily impressions." The fivefold sense activity, however, is already suspended in the first *jhāna*.

"What are here the perceptions of diversity (*nānatta-saññā*)? They are the perception, or the perceiving, or the having perceived and experienced by anyone outside the *jhānas*, in whom the mind-element (*mano-dhātu*) or mind-consciousness element (*manoviññāṇa-dhātu*: see §157) is active" (Vibh XII,604).

"'Boundless is space!' means that the monk directs his mind to that space, fixes it therein, and pervades it as boundless" (Vibh XII,605).

§122 (2) Sphere of Boundless Consciousness (*viññāṇañcāyatana*)

Through the total overcoming of the sphere of boundless space, and with the idea: "Unbounded is consciousness," he reaches the sphere of boundless consciousness and abides therein.

"'Boundless consciousness' means that the monk gives attention to that same space pervaded by consciousness, and thus pervades it as boundless" (Vibh XII,610).

"In order to reach this state, he should again and again consider the consciousness pervading that space, pay attention to it, contemplate it, thrash it out over and over with his mind (while in the sensuous sphere).... Now, while again and again directing his mind to the object of contemplation, his hindrances (*nīvaraṇa*) become suppressed, his attentiveness becomes firm, and his mind reaches neighbourhood concentration (*upacāra-samādhi*). However, he practises, develops, and cultivates that object, and in doing so, the consciousness of the sphere of boundless consciousness reaches absorption concentration (*appanā-samādhi*)" (Vism X,25).

§123 (3) Sphere of Nothingness (*ākiñcaññāyatana*)

Through the total overcoming of the sphere of boundless consciousness, and with the idea: "Nothing is there," he reaches the sphere of nothingness and abides therein.

In order to reach this state, the monk pays full attention to the nothingness and emptiness of that consciousness of boundless space, which has the sphere of boundless space as object. However, paying no more attention to the sphere of boundless consciousness, he again and again considers the idea: "Nothing is there! Nothing is there!" or "Empty is this! Empty is this!" etc. Now, while keeping the mind directed to that idea, and while all mental hindrances disappear in him, his attentiveness becomes firm, and his mind reaches neighbourhood concentration. Again and again practising and developing this subject of contemplation, the consciousness of the sphere of nothingness reaches full development with regard to the emptiness and hollowness of the consciousness arisen through the pervasion of space. (See Vism X, 32–34.)

In Vibh XII,615 it is said: "'Nothing is there' means: The monk brings that consciousness (of boundless space) to non-existence, to cessation, to disappearance."

§124

(4) Sphere of Neither-Perception-Nor-Nonperception

(*neva-saññā-n' āsaññāyatana*)

Through the total overcoming of the sphere of nothingness he reaches the sphere of neither-perception-nor-nonperception.

This state also is reached in a similar way. In Vibh XII,619 it is said: "He considers that sphere of nothingness as peaceful, and thereafter he develops the attainment of the last remainder of mental factors (as perception, feeling, volition, etc., which are all on the verge of cessation)."

Though the monk considers the sphere of nothingness as peaceful, he nevertheless turns his mind away from it and directs it to the sphere of neither-perception-nor-nonperception, as this state is still more peaceful and sublime.

The name of this state is meant to convey the idea that one cannot speak any more of "perception" in the ordinary sense, but that, correctly speaking, there still remains an infinitesimal degree of perception. This, however, holds good for all the remaining mental factors, as feeling, volition, consciousness, etc., so that one could speak just as well of "neither-feeling-nor-nonfeeling," or "neither-consciousness-nor-nonconsciousness," etc.

Thus, of the four immaterial spheres, the first arises through overcoming perceptions of forms, the second through overcoming the idea of space, the third through overcoming the idea of consciousness, the fourth through overcoming the idea of absence of consciousness of space.

§125 Perception of Loathsomeness of food
(āhāra-paṭikūla-saññā)

Of the four kinds of nutrition only material food is meant here. Vism XI,5 says one has to practise this contemplation with regard to the loathsomeness of secretion of bile, phlegm, pus, and blood, the loathsomeness of the depository in the body, the loathsomeness of the undigested and digested food, the excretions, etc.

AN 7:46

The perception of loathsomeness of food, O monks, developed and frequently carried out, brings high reward and blessing, has the Deathless as support and goal. In what regard has this been said?

Whoever, O monks, often entertains the perception of loathsomeness of food, his mind shrinks back from gluttony, turns away from it, feels aversion, is not attracted; and equanimity or disgust is present.

Just as, O monks, a cock's feather or a piece of bowstring, thrown into the fire, shrinks up, twists, rolls itself up, does not stretch out again: just so in one who often entertains the perception of loathsomeness of food, the mind shrinks back from gluttony, turns away from it, feels aversion, is not attracted; and equanimity or disgust is present.

SN 46:69

Once, O monks, the perception of loathsomeness of food has been developed and frequently carried out, it will bring great reward and blessing—and one may expect one of two results: highest wisdom in this very life or, if a remainder of clinging is left, never-return, and it leads to great well-being—to great peace of heart—to emotion—to happiness. And how so?

Herein the monk develops the seven factors of enlightenment accompanied by the perception of loathsomeness of food, based on seclusion, detachment, and cessation, and leading to abandonment, namely: mindfulness, investigation of the truth, energy, rapture, tranquillity, concentration, and equanimity.

SN 12:63

How, O monks, is material food to be regarded? Let us say, O monks, two persons, husband and wife, with only few provisions, are wandering through a desert. With them is their only child, their beloved and dear little son. But now, while they are in the midst of the desert, their few provisions grow less and less and come to an end, but they have not yet crossed the remainder of the desert.

And both, husband and wife, consider thus: "Now, our few provisions have been eaten up and have drawn to an end, but we have not yet crossed the remainder of the desert. Now, let us kill our only child, our beloved dear little son, prepare dried and seasoned meat, and thus, eating the flesh of our child, we will cross the remaining portion of the desert, so that not all three of us perish."

And both killed their only beloved child, their dear little son, prepared dried and seasoned meat, and thus, eating their own child's flesh, crossed the remaining portion of the desert. But, while eating the flesh, they beat their breasts, weeping and lamenting: "Where is our own little son now? Where is our only child?"

What do you think, O monks: do those two people eat their food for amusement, or for pleasure, or to become handsome and beautiful?

"No, O Venerable One."

Did they not eat their food only to escape the desert?

"Indeed, O Venerable One."

Just so, O monks, should one regard material food: thus I say. Once one has fully understood material food, one has fully understood the greed for the five sense objects. But once one has fully understood the greed for the five sense objects, there exists no more any fetter bound by which the noble disciple should ever return again to this world.

§127 **The Early Teachers**

(cited at Vism XI,23)

The pleasant drink, the pleasant food,
Hard, soft, whatever it may be:
Through one door it is loaded in,
Through nine it trickles out again.

The pleasant drink, the pleasant food,
Hard, soft, whatever it may be:
Man may in company enjoy,
Yet, in discharging it, he hides.

The pleasant drink, the pleasant food,
Hard, soft, whatever it may be:
Man may enjoy with full delight,
Yet, in discharging, feels disgust.

The pleasant drink, the pleasant food,
Hard, soft, whatever it may be:
The whole, after one single night,
Will reach a state of loathsomeness.

AN 5:30

Truly, Nāgita, whatever has been eaten, drunk, chewed, and tasted, all will end in excrement and urine: such is the outcome.

§128 Analysis of the four elements
(dhātu-vavatthāna)

This exercise is handed down in condensed form in MN 10 and DN 22; in detailed form in MN 28, 62, 140. The four elements, of which all gross as well as fine-material phenomena consist, are:

(1) "earth element" or the solid (*paṭhavi-dhātu*)
(2) "water element" or the liquid (*āpo-dhātu*)
(3) "fire element" or heat (*tejo-dhātu*)
(4) "wind element" or motion (*vāyo-dhātu*)

In Vism XI,84 the four elements are defined thus: Whatever is characterized by hardness (*thaddha-lakkhaṇa*) is the earth or solid element; by "binding together" or cohesion (*ābandhana*), the water element; by "heating" (*paripācana*), the fire or heat element; by "strengthening" (*vitthambhana*), the wind or motion element.

MN 28

1. What now is the solid element? It may be one's own, or it may be external. And what is one's own solid element? Whatever there is, in one's own person and body, of hard and solid things karmically acquired, such as head-hairs, body-hairs, nails, teeth, etc.: this is called one's own solid element. Now, whether it be one's own solid element, or the external solid element, they are both only the solid element.

And one should understand, according to reality and true wisdom: "This does not belong to me; this am I not; this is not my self."

2. What now is the fluid element? It may be one's own, or it may be external. And what is one's own fluid element? Whatever there is in one's own person and body, of watery and cohesive things karmically acquired, such as bile, phlegm, pus, blood, etc.: this is called one's own fluid element. Now, whether it be one's own fluid element, or the external fluid element, they are both only the fluid element....

3. What now is the heat element? It may be one's own, or it may be external. And what is one's own heat element? Whatever there is in one's own person and body, of heating and radiating things karmically acquired, as that whereby one's body is heated, consumed, and scorched, whereby that which has been eaten, drunk, chewed, or tasted is fully digested, etc.: this is called one's own heat element. Now, whether it be one's own heat element, or the external heat element, they are both only the heat element....

4. What now is the wind element? It may be one's own, or it may be external. And what is one's own wind element? Whatever there is in one's own person and body, of mobile and gaseous things karmically acquired, such as the upward-going and downward-going winds, the winds of stomach and intestines, in-breathing and out-breathing, etc.: this is called one's own wind element. Now, whether it be one's own wind element, or the external wind element, they are both only the wind element.

And one should understand, according to reality and true wisdom: "This does not belong to me; this am I not; this is not my self."

THE FOUR APPLICATIONS OF MINDFULNESS
(*satipaṭṭhāna*)

§129 MN 10; DN 22

Satipaṭṭhāna (=*sati-upaṭṭhāna*) literally means "the setting up of mindfulness" or presence of mindfulness. There are four applications of mindfulness: contemplation of the body, of the feelings, of mind, and of mind-objects. They are illustrated by a number of very significant concentration exercises and insight exercises, so that all Buddhists rightly consider this sutta the most important portion of the whole Sutta Piṭaka and the quintessence of the whole meditation practice.

Once the Blessed One dwelt in the country of the Kurus, near the little market town called Kammāsa-damma. There the Blessed One addressed the monks: "Monks." "Venerable

One!" replied those monks to the Blessed One. And the Blessed One said:

The only way that leads to the attainment of purity, to the overcoming of sorrow and lamentation, to the end of pain and grief, to the entering upon the right path, and to the realization of Nibbāna, is the four applications of mindfulness. And which are these four?

Herein the monk dwells in contemplation of the body, of feelings, of mind, and of mind-objects, ardent, clearly conscious and mindful, after putting away worldly greed and grief.

1. Contemplation of the Body

But how does the monk dwell in contemplation of the body? Herein the monk retires to the forest, to the foot of a tree, or to a solitary place, sits down, with legs crossed, body erect, and with mindfulness fixed before him.

(*In-and-out breathing*): Mindful he breathes in, mindful he breathes out. When making a long inhalation, he knows: "I make a long inhalation"; when making a long exhalation, he knows: "I make a long exhalation," etc.

For details see §§92–93.

(*Four postures*): And further, while going, standing, sitting, or lying, the monk understands (according to reality) the expressions: "*I* go"; "*I* stand"; "*I* sit"; "*I* lie down." He understands any position of the body.

> The monk understands that there is no living being, no real ego, that goes, stands, etc., but that it is by a mere figure of speech that one says: "I go," "I stand," etc.

(*Mindfulness and clear consciousness*): And further, the monk is clearly conscious in going and coming; clearly conscious in looking forward and backward; clearly conscious in bending forward and stretching; clearly conscious in eating, drinking, chewing, and tasting; clearly conscious in discharging excrement and urine; clearly conscious in walking, standing, sitting, falling asleep, and awakening; clearly conscious in speaking and keeping silent.

(*Loathsomeness*): And further, the monk contemplates this body, from the soles of the feet upward, and from the top of the hair downward, etc.

For details see §§90–91.

(*Elements*): And further, the monk contemplates this body with regard to the elements: "This body consists of the solid, fluid, heating, and windy elements." Just as a skilled butcher or butcher's apprentice, who has slaughtered a cow and divided it into separate portions, might sit down at the junction of four highroads; just so does the monk contemplate this body with regard to the elements.

For details see §128; B. Dict.: *dhātuvavatthāna.*

(*Cemetery*): And further, just as if the monk should see a corpse thrown into the burial ground, one, two, or three days dead, swollen up, blue-black in colour, full of corruption ...

- a corpse eaten by crows, hawks, or vultures ...
- a framework of bones, flesh hanging from it, bespattered with blood, held together by the sinews ...
- a framework of bones, stripped of flesh, bespattered with blood, held together by the sinews ...
- a framework of bones, without flesh and blood, but still held together by the sinews ...
- bones disconnected and scattered in all directions ...
- bones bleached and resembling shells ...
- bones heaped together, after the lapse of years ...
- bones weathered and crumbled to dust; he draws the conclusion as to his own body: "This my body too has this nature, this destiny, and cannot escape it."

See §80

Thus he dwells in contemplation with regard to his own body and external bodies. He beholds how the body arises, or how it passes away, or how it arises and passes away. "A body is there": this clear consciousness is present in him, because of his knowledge and mindfulness; and he lives independent, unattached to anything in the world. Thus the monk dwells in contemplation of the body.

> The monk knows: "A body is there, but no living being, no individual, no woman, no man, no self, nothing that belongs to a self; neither a person, nor anything belonging to a person" (Comy.).

2. Contemplation of Feelings

But how does the monk dwell in contemplation of the feelings?

In experiencing feelings, the monk knows: "I have an agreeable feeling ... a disagreeable feeling ... an indifferent feeling ... a worldly agreeable feeling ... an unworldly agreeable feeling ... a worldly disagreeable feeling ... an unworldly disagreeable feeling ... a worldly indifferent feeling ... an unworldly indifferent feeling."

Thus he dwells in contemplation with regard to his own feelings, or the feelings of others, or the feelings of both. He beholds how feelings arise, or how they pass away, or how they arise and pass away. "Feelings are there": this clear consciousness is present in him, because of his knowledge and mindfulness; and he lives independent, unattached to anything in the world. Thus the monk dwells in contemplation of feelings.

> The monk understands that the expression "I feel" has no validity except as an expression of "common speech" (*vohāra-vacana*), and that in the "ultimate sense" (*paramattha*) there are only feelings, but no ego, no person, no experiencer of the feelings.

3. Contemplation of Mind

But how does the monk dwell in contemplation of the mind? Herein the monk knows when the mind is greedy or not greedy, angry or not angry, deluded or undeluded, cramped or scattered, developed or undeveloped, surpassable or unsurpassable, concentrated or unconcentrated, freed or unfreed....

Thus he dwells in contemplation with regard to his own mind, or the mind of others, or the mind of both. He beholds how the mind arises, or how it passes away, or how it arises and passes away. "Mind is there": this clear consciousness is present in him, because of his knowledge and mindfulness; and he lives independent, unattached to anything in the world. Thus the monk dwells in contemplation of the mind.

4. Contemplation of Mind-Objects

(*Five hindrances*): But how does the monk dwell in contemplation of the mind-objects? Herein the monk dwells in contemplation of the mind-objects, such as the five hindrances. He knows when there is sensual lust in him ... anger ... torpor and drowsiness ... restlessness and worry ... sceptical doubt, or when these things are not in him ... knows how they come to arise; knows how, once arisen, they are overcome; knows how, once overcome, they do not arise again in the future.

(*Five groups*): And further, the monk knows what corporeality ... feeling ... perception ... mental formations ... consciousness is, how it arises, and how it passes away....

(*Six bases*): And further, the monk knows eye and visible objects ... ear and sounds ... nose and odours ... tongue and tastes ... body and body-impressions ... mind and mind-objects: and he knows the fetter that arises in dependence on them; knows how the fetter is overcome, and how the abandoned fetter does not arise again in the future.

(*Seven factors of enlightenment*): The monk knows when there is mindfulness in him ... investigation of the Dhamma ... energy ... rapture ... tranquillity ... concentration ... equanimity; knows when these things are not in him ... knows how they come to arise, and how they are fully developed.

(*Four Noble Truths*): The monk knows according to reality what suffering is ... the origin of suffering ... the cessation of suffering ... the path that leads to the cessation of suffering.

Thus he dwells in contemplation of the mind-objects, either with regard to his own person, or to other persons, or to both. He beholds how the mind-objects arise, or how they pass away, or how they arise and pass away. "Mind-objects are there": this clear consciousness is present in him because of his knowledge and mindfulness; and he lives independent, unattached to anything in the world. Thus the monk dwells in contemplation of the mind-objects.

The only way that leads to the attainment of purity, to the overcoming of sorrow and lamentation, to the end of pain and grief, to the entering upon the right path and the realization of Nibbāna, is these four applications of mindfulness.

§130 The Eight deliverances

(*aṭṭha vimokkha*)
AN 8:66; DN 33

There are eight deliverances, O monks. And which are these?

(1) While endowed with corporeal form (*rūpī*) one perceives forms; this is the first deliverance.

(2) Not perceiving forms on one's own person, one perceives forms externally: that is the second deliverance.

(3) By thinking of the beautiful, one is filled with confidence: this is the third deliverance.

(4) Through the total overcoming of the perceptions of forms, through the vanishing of the reflex perceptions, and through non-attention to the perceptions of diversity, with the idea "Boundless is space," one reaches the sphere of boundless space and abides therein: this is the fourth deliverance.

(5) Through the total overcoming of the sphere of boundless space, and with the idea "Boundless is consciousness," one reaches the sphere of boundless consciousness and abides therein: this is the fifth deliverance.

(6) Through the total overcoming of the sphere of boundless consciousness, and with the idea "Nothing is there," one reaches the sphere of nothingness and abides therein; this is the sixth deliverance.

(7) Through the total overcoming of the sphere of nothingness, one reaches the sphere of neither-perception-nor-nonperception and abides therein; this is the seventh deliverance.

(8) Through the total overcoming of the sphere of neither-perception-nor-nonperception one reaches the cessation of perception and abides therein; this is the eighth deliverance.

These, O monks, are the eight kinds of deliverance.

About 1–3 see §78 and B. Dict.: *abhibhāyatana*; about 4–7 see §119–24.

§131 Ten Contemplations

(*Girimānanda Sutta*)

AN 10:60

Once the Blessed One dwelt in the Jeta Grove near Sāvatthī, in the monastery of Anāthapiṇḍika. Now at that time the Venerable Girimānanda was sick, suffering, attacked by a serious disease. And the Venerable Ānanda went to the Blessed One, saluted him reverentially, and sitting on one side said:

"The Venerable Girimānanda, O Venerable One, is sick, suffering, attacked by a serious disease. It would be good if the Venerable One, out of compassion, would go to see him."

If you, Ānanda, would go to the monk Girimānanda and recite to him ten contemplations (*saññā*), it may be that, after he has heard them, the monk Girimānanda's illness will stop at once. And which are these ten contemplations? They are: the contemplations of impermanence, of non-self, of loathsomeness, of misery, of overcoming, of detachment, of extinction, of the unattractiveness of the whole world, of the impermanence of all formations, and mindfulness of in-and-out breathing.

But what, Ānanda, is the contemplation of impermanence? Here the monk goes to the forest, to the foot of a tree, or to an empty hut and considers thus: "Corporeality is impermanent, feeling is impermanent, perception is impermanent, the mental formations are impermanent, consciousness is impermanent." Thus he dwells in the contemplation of the impermanence of the five groups forming the objects of clinging. This is called the contemplation of impermanence.

§132 But what, Ānanda, is the contemplation of non-self? Here the monk considers thus: "The eye and visible forms are non-self, ear and sounds ... nose and odours ... tongue and tastes ... body and body-impressions ... mind and mind-objects are non-self." Thus he dwells in the contemplation of non-self with regard to these six internal and external bases. This is called the contemplation of non-self.

§133 But what, Ānanda, is the contemplation of loathsomeness? Here the monk contemplates this body from the soles of the feet upward, and from the top of the hair downward, with a skin stretched over it, and filled with many impurities: "This body consists of head-hairs, body-hairs, nails, teeth, skin, flesh, sinews, bones, marrow, kidneys, heart, liver, diaphragm, spleen, lungs, intestines, mesentery.... This is called the contemplation of loathsomeness.

For details see §§ 90–91.

§134 But what, Ānanda, is the contemplation of misery? Here the monk considers thus: "Truly, full of sickness is this body, full of misery. Many kinds of suffering arise in this body, such as: diseases of eye, ear, nose, tongue, body, head, shell of the ear, mouth, teeth, cough, asthma, nasal catarrh, inner heat, fever, belly ache, swoon, diarrhoea, pricking, cholera, leprosy, swelling, skin eruption, consumption, epilepsy, scurvy, scabies, scurf, demoniac possession, bilious disease, diabetes, palsy (piles?), boils, fistula, diseases brought about by bile, phlegm, gases or their combination, due to climatic changes, irregular living or accidents, or due to karma; further cold, heat, hunger, thirst, excrement, and urine." Thus he dwells in contemplation of the misery of this body. This is called the contemplation of misery.

§135 But what, Ānanda, is the contemplation of overcoming? Here the monk does not allow a thought of lust, ill-will, or cruelty, or any other arisen evil and unwholesome mental states, to gain a footing; he overcomes them, dispels them, destroys them, annihilates them. This is called the contemplation of overcoming.

§136 But what, Ānanda, is the contemplation of detachment? In that case the monk retires to the forest, the foot of a tree, or an empty hut and considers thus: "This is peace, this is the sublime, namely, the standstill of all karma-formations, the abandoning of all substrata of existence, the vanishing of craving, detachment, Nibbāna." This is called the contemplation of detachment.

§137 But what, Ānanda, is the contemplation of cessation? Here the monk considers thus: "This is peace, this is the sublime, namely, the standstill of all karma-formations, the abandoning of all substrata of existence, the vanishing of craving, cessation, Nibbāna." This is called the contemplation of cessation.

§138 But what, Ānanda, is the contemplation of the unattractiveness of the whole world? Whatever exists in the mind of an inclination and clinging to this world, of proclivity, adherence, and bias, all this the monk abandons, keeps away from it, does not cling to it. This is called the contemplation of the unattractiveness of the whole world.

§139 But what, Ānanda, is the contemplation of the impermanence of all formations? Here the monk feels horror, disgust, and aversion with regard to all formations. This is called the contemplation of the impermanence of all formations.

§140 But what, Ānanda, is mindfulness of in-and-out breathing? Here the monk retires to the forest, the foot of a tree, or an empty hut, sits down cross-legged, body erect, his mindfulness fixed before him. Mindfully he breathes in, mindfully he breathes out. This is called mindfulness of in-and-out breathing.

Here follow the sixteen breathing exercises which are given in detail at §92.

Having heard these ten contemplations from the Blessed One, the Venerable Ānanda went to the Venerable Girimānanda and recited these ten contemplations to him. Then as soon as the Venerable Girimānanda heard these ten contemplations, his illness at once subsided. And the Venerable Girimānanda rose from his sick-bed, and his illness was overcome.

§141 **Overcoming and Developing**

AN 6:107–16

The idea of loathsomeness (of the body) must be developed to overcome greed; all-embracing kindness, to overcome hatred; wisdom, to overcome delusion.

Good conduct in deeds, words, and thoughts must be developed to overcome bad conduct in deeds, words, and thoughts.

The thought of renunciation must be developed to overcome sensual thought, hateless thought to overcome hateful thoughts, harmless thought to overcome cruel thoughts ... the idea of impermanence to overcome happiness belief, the idea of non-self to overcome view of self, right views to overcome wrong views, altruistic joy to overcome ill-humour, harmlessness to overcome cruelty, right conduct to overcome wrong conduct, contentedness to overcome discontentedness, mental clarity to overcome mental confusion, frugality to overcome avarice, mild manners to overcome rude manners, good companionship to overcome bad companionship, mindfulness of in-and-out breathing to overcome mental distractedness, mental tranquillity to overcome restlessness, mental control to overcome lack of control, vigilance to overcome negligence.

§142 **The SIX spiritual powers**

(*abhiññā*)

These are:

(1) psychic powers (*iddhi*),
(2) the divine ear (*dibba-sota*),
(3) penetrating the hearts of others (*cetopariya-ñāṇa*)

(4) remembering former births (*pubbe nivāsānussati*),
(5) the divine eye (*dibba-cakkhu*),
(6) the cessation of all taints (*āsavakkhaya*).

(1–5) are mundane (*lokiya*) and, like the *jhānas*, not necessary for attaining deliverance, while (6) is supramundane (*lokuttara*) and identical with the path and fruit of arahatship; (4–6) are also known as the threefold wisdom (*tevijjā*).

The first five spiritual powers (*abhiññā*) are the result of extraordinary spiritual training. To gain these, one should first master the four *jhānas*, of which the fourth *jhāna* forms the foundation (*pādaka-jhāna*) for the five spiritual powers. Their real purpose should be to facilitate the development of insight (*vipassanā*). For detailed explanations, see Vism XII, XIII.

AN 5:23

§143 There are five mental defilements, O monks, defiled by which the mind is neither pliable nor supple nor limpid, but unyielding and not well directed to the cessation of the taints (*āsavakkhaya*). And which are these five?

They are: sensual lust, ill-will, torpor and languor, restlessness and worry, and sceptical doubt. As soon, however, as the mind is freed from these five defilements (usually called "mental hindrances"; see §129, 4), it is pliable, supple, limpid, no longer unyielding, and well directed to the cessation of the taints. Now, to whichever of the phenomena attainable through wisdom one directs the mind for comprehending them wisely, herein one will attain the faculty of comprehending them, whenever the conditions are present.

For full details, see B. Dict.: *abhiññā.*

3
WISDOM
(*paññā*)

3
Wisdom
(paññā)

General Remarks

§144 Now we come to the third stage on the path to deliverance, namely the development of wisdom (paññā-bhāvanā). The specific Buddhist wisdom pertaining to the Eightfold Path is the insight-wisdom (vipassanā-paññā) which, like lightning, suddenly arises and penetrates to the true nature of all existence, i.e. the impermanence, unsatisfactoriness, and selflessness (anicca, dukkha, anattā) of those five groups of phenomena (khandha) constituting existence, namely: corporeality, feeling, perception, mental formations, and consciousness. And only this penetrating insight-wisdom, fully developed, leads to the immediate attaining of the four supramundane paths of stream entry, once-return, non-return, and arahatship (see B. Dict.: ariya-puggala).

In Vism XIV,7 it is said: "Wisdom has as characteristic the penetrating of the nature of things. Its essence (function) consists in dispelling the darkness of ignorance that veils the true nature of things. Its manifestation consists in undeludedness, its foundation is concentration (samādhi) according to the words: 'One whose mind is concentrated knows and sees things according to reality.'"

With regard to the sources of wisdom, one distinguishes three kinds, according to the following text:

§145 **Three Kinds of Wisdom**

DN 33

There are three kinds of wisdom: wisdom due to one's own thinking (*cintā-mayā-paññā*); wisdom due to instruction (*suta-mayā-paññā*); wisdom due to mental development (*bhāvanā-mayā-paññā*).

Vibh XVI, 768 explains: "What now is the wisdom due to one's own thinking? Be it in the way of some work, or of art, or science, be it the true conception, view, confidence, opinion, understanding or fondness of the truth that teaches that corporeality, etc., are impermanent, unsatisfactory, non-self: such wisdom is due to one's own thinking. If, however, it has been learnt from others, it is called wisdom due to instruction, while the wisdom of one who has entered *jhāna* is called the wisdom due to mental development."

Only the insight-wisdom associated with the four kinds of supramundane path- and fruit-consciousness, is called "supramundane" (*lokuttara*); any other wisdom is "mundane" (*lokiya*).

The objects of insight-wisdom are:

1. the five groups of existence (*khandha*; see §§146–53),
2. the twelve bases (*āyatana*; see §§154–56),
3. the eighteen elements (*dhātu*; see §157),
4. the twenty-two faculties (*indriya*; see §§158–62),
5. the Four Noble Truths (*sacca*; see §§163–67),
6. dependent origination (*paṭicca-samuppāda*; see §§168–75).

§146 The Five groups of existence

(*pañca khandha*)

SN 22:48

What, O monks, are the five groups of existence? Whatever there are of corporeal things, past, present, or future, one's own or external, gross or subtle, lofty or low, far or near, that all belongs to the corporeality group. Whatever there is of feeling ... of perception ... of mental formations ... of consciousness ... all that belongs to the consciousness group.

SN 5:10

When certain things we find combined,
We speak of "chariot," speak of "car."
Just so, when these five groups appear,
We use the designation "a being."

SN 22:95

Suppose a man with good sight were to behold the many bubbles on the Ganges as they are driving along; and he should watch them and carefully examine them. After he has carefully examined them, they will appear to him empty, unreal, and unsubstantial. In exactly the same way does the monk behold all corporeal phenomena, feelings, perceptions, mental formations, and consciousness, whether past, present, or future, one's own or external, gross or subtle, lofty or low, far or near. And he watches them, and examines them carefully; and, after he has carefully examined them, they appear to him empty, unreal, and unsubstantial.

The body is like a lump of foam,
The feelings like a water bubble,
Perception like a void mirage,
Formations like a plantain tree,
And consciousness like jugglery.

§147 SN 22:56

I. But what, O monks, is the corporeality group (*rūpakkhandha*)? It is the four primary elements and the corporeality depending on them.

The four elements (*dhātu*) are: the solid, liquid, heat, and motion elements (see §128).

Dependent corporeality (*upādā-rūpa*) consists of:

(1–5) five physical sense organs;

(6–9) physical objects of seeing, hearing, smelling, and tasting. The objects of body-impression are not enumerated here, as they are identical with the already mentioned solid, heat, and motion elements recognizable through the sensations of pressure, touch, cold, heat, pain, etc.;

(10, 11) femininity, virility;

(12) physical vitality (*jīvitindriya*);

(13) physical base of mind (see B. Dict. *hadaya-vatthu*);

(14–15) bodily and verbal expression (*kāya-viññatti, vacī-viññatti*);

(16) space (delimitation);

(17–23) bodily agility, plasticity, tractability, growth, continuity, decay, impermanence;

(24) nutriment.

§148 II. But what, O monks, is the feeling group (*vedanā-kkhandha*)? There are six kinds of feelings: feeling due to visual impression, to sound impression, to smell impression, to taste impression, to body impression, to mind-impression.

The threefold (or fivefold) division is: (bodily or mental) pleasant feeling, (bodily or mental) painful feeling, indifferent feeling. Cf. §160.

§149 III. But what, O monks, is the perception group (*saññā-kkhandha*)? There are six kinds of perception: perception of visible forms, sounds, odours, tastes, bodily impressions, and mind-objects.

§150 IV. But what, O monks, is the mental formations group (*saṅkhāra-kkhandha*)? There are six kinds of volitions (*cetanā*): regarding visible forms, sounds, odours, tastes, bodily impressions, and mind-objects.

In Vism XIV,125-84 fifty-two mental factors, or concomitants of consciousness (*cetasika*), are enumerated. Of these, as shown above, feeling and perception are counted as separate groups, while the remaining fifty mental factors, led by volition (*cetanā*, i.e. *saṅkhāra*), are collectively taken as the "group of mental formations."

These consist of :

11 general ones, i.e.

5 primary, inseparably associated with all consciousness: impression, volition, mental vitality, concentration, and advertence (*manasikāra*).

6 secondary, occasionally associated: thought conception, discursive thinking, determination, energy, interest, and intention.

24 lofty ones, i.e.
19 primary: faith, mindfulness, moral shame, conscience, greedlessness, etc.
6 secondary, occasionally associated: compassion, altruistic joy, wisdom, abstaining from bad deeds, bad speech, and bad livelihood.
14 karmically unwholesome ones, i.e.
4 primary, associated with all unwholesome consciousness: delusion, shamelessness, unconscientiousness, and restlessness.
10 secondary, occasionally associated: hate, envy, stinginess, worry, greed, wrong view, conceit, torpor, languor, and sceptical doubt.

§151 V. But what, O monks, is the consciousness group (*viññāṇa-kkhandha*)? There are six kinds of consciousness: eye-consciousness, ear-consciousness, nose-consciousness, tongue-consciousness, body-consciousness, and mind-consciousness.

In regard to karma, consciousness is divided into three classes:

1. karmically wholesome consciousness (*kusala-citta* or *viññāṇa*).
2. karmically unwholesome consciousness (*akusala-citta* or *viññāṇa*).
3. karmically neutral consciousness (*avyākata-citta* or *viññāṇa*).

(1) and (2) are associated with either wholesome or unwholesome action in deeds, words, or thoughts.

To (3) belong the five kinds of sense-consciousness (seeing, hearing, etc.) which, according to the desirability or undesirability of their objects, are to be understood as the result of wholesome or unwholesome karma, or volitional action.

About the five groups and the combination of the mental concomitants with consciousness, Vism. XIV, Dhs, and Abhs give detailed explanations. See also Guide, and B. Dict., and the Table in both books.

§152 Dependent Origination of the Five Groups

MN 28

Now, though one's eye be intact, yet if external visible forms do not fall within the field of vision, and no corresponding conjunction of eye and forms takes place, in that case there occurs no formation of the corresponding aspect of consciousness. Or, though one's eye be intact, and external forms fall within the field of vision, yet if no corresponding conjunction takes place, in that case too there occurs no formation of the corresponding aspect of consciousness. If, however, one's eye is intact, and external forms fall within the field of vision, and the corresponding conjunction takes place, in that case there arises the corresponding aspect of consciousness.

Whatever on such an occasion there exists of corporeality, that belongs to the corporeality group; whatever exists of feeling, that belongs to the feeling group; whatever exists of perception, that belongs to the perception group; whatever exists of mental formations, that belongs to the mental formations group; whatever exists of consciousness, that belongs to the consciousness group.... This has been said by the Blessed One: "One who sees dependent origination, sees the Dhamma and one who sees the Dhamma, sees dependent origination." These five groups of existence are dependently arisen.

§153 Inseparability of the Mental Groups

MN 43

"Whatever, O brother, there is of feeling, perception, and consciousness, are these things associated one with another, or are they dissociated; and is it possible to separate them one by one and show their difference?"

"Whatever there is of feeling, perception, and consciousness, these things are associated with each other, not dissociated; and it is not possible to separate them one by one and show their difference. Whatever one feels, that one perceives; and whatever one perceives, of that one is conscious. Hence these things are associated, not dissociated; and it is not possible to separate them one by one and show their difference.

SN 22:54

If, O monks, consciousness continues to be directed towards corporeality, is based on corporeality, supported by it and accompanied by inclination to pleasure, then consciousness will come to growth, increase, and development. If consciousness continues to be directed towards feeling ... perception ... mental formations, is based thereon, supported thereby and accompanied by inclination to pleasure, then consciousness will come to growth, increase, and development.

§154 The Twelve Bases
(āyatana)

The twelve bases, or fundamental conditions of all mental processes, consist of the five physical sense organs and the corresponding five external physical sense objects, while the sixth is consciousness, the twelfth a physical or mental object:

1. visual organ (eye)	7. visible form
2. acoustic organ (ear)	8. sound
3. olfactory organ (nose)	9. odour
4. gustatory organ (tongue)	10. taste
5. bodily organ (body)	11. bodily impression
6. mind organ	12. mind-object (dhamma)

§155 DN 33

There are six internal bases: eye, ear, nose, tongue, body, and mind-base; and there are six external bases: form, sound, odour, taste, bodily impression, and mind-object.

For details see Guide II (ii) or B. Dict. *āyatana.* The physical organs refer here to their respective particular sensitivity and not, e.g., to the entire eyeball, etc.

"The visible object (*rūpa*) is that physical phenomenon that corresponds to the visual organ and appears as blue, yellow, red, light, dark, and conditioned by which, dependent on the visual organ, visual impression, etc., arise" (Dhs § 617—20).

Mind-base (*manāyatana*) is a collective term for the five classes of sense consciousness, the mind-element (*manodhātu*; s. §157), and mind-consciousness-element (*manoviññāṇa-dhātu*; s. §157). "Subconsciousness" (*bhavaṅga-citta*) is included in this base and is considered the "door of mind" (*manodvāra*), while the five physical sense organs are the doors for the five kinds of sense consciousness.

§156 MN 38

The arising of consciousness is dependent upon conditions; and without these conditions no consciousness ever arises. And upon whatever conditions the arising of consciousness is dependent, after these it is called.

If the arising of consciousness is dependent on eye and form, it is called eye-consciousness; if on ear and sound: ear-consciousness; if on nose and odour: nose-consciousness; if on tongue and taste: tongue-consciousness; if on body and bodily impression: body-consciousness; if on mind and mind-object: mind-consciousness.

SN 35:197

"Empty village," O monks, is a name for the six internal sense bases. When a monk, a wise, learned, prudent man, examines these bases with regard to eye, ear, nose, tongue, body, and eye, ear, nose, tongue, body, and mind, then these things appear to him perfectly desolate, vain, and empty.

"Village robbers," O monks, is a name for the six external bases. For the eye, O monks, is attacked by pleasant and unpleasant forms, the ear by pleasant and unpleasant sounds, the nose by pleasant and unpleasant odours ... the mind by pleasant and unpleasant mind-objects.

§157 The Eighteen Elements

(*dhātu*)

MN 115

There are, Ānanda, eighteen elements:

1. eye	10.taste
2. ear	11.bodily impression
3. nose	12.mind-object (*dhamma*)
4. tongue	13.eye-consciousness
5. body	14.ear-consciousness
6. mind-element (*manodhātu*)	15.nose-consciousness
7. visible form	16.tongue-consciousness
8. sound	17.body-consciousness
9. odour (*mano-viññāṇa*)	18.mind-consciousness

(1–5) and (7–12) are identical with the corresponding eleven bases. "Mind-element" (6), however, is not identical with "mind base," but is only that conscious element that performs the function of advertence (*āvajjana*) and reception (*sampaṭicchana*) of the sense object (see Table 39, 55, 70 in B. Dict.). (18) in its widest sense, comprises all consciousness except mind element and the five kinds of sense consciousness.

Mind element is always associated with thought conception and discursive thinking (*vitakka-vicāra*), while the mind-consciousness element is sometimes free from it (e.g. in the *jhānas* beyond the first).

Two elements, namely, mind-consciousness and mind-object, may be either karmically wholesome (*kusala*), unwholesome (*akusala*), or neutral (*avyākata*).

According to Vism XV,39, the arising of the six kinds of sense consciousness is explained by the Early Masters thus: "Conditioned by eye, visual object, light, and mental advertence (*āvajjana*), eye-consciousness arises.... Conditioned by ear, sound, ear-drum, and mental advertence, ear-consciousness arises. ... Conditioned by nose, olfactory object, air, and mental advertence, nose-consciousness arises.... Conditioned by tongue, gustatory object, humidity, and mental advertence, tongue-consciousness arises....

Conditioned by body, body-impression, earth element, and mental advertence, body-consciousness arises.... Conditioned by subconsciousness (*bhavaṅga-mano*), mind-object, and mental advertence, mind-consciousness arises."

About the process of sense-perception, see Guide II (iii).

It may be stated here that the eighteen elements, like the twelve bases, comprise everything mental and corporeal, in other words, the whole world.

§158 The Twenty-Two Faculties
(*indriya*)

There are twenty-two faculties, partly physical, partly mental or ethical, which are enumerated and explained in the Suttas and Abhidhamma; only the last three supramundane faculties are merely enumerated in the Suttas, but not explained. They are:

1. eye
2. ear
3. nose
4. tongue
5. body
6. mind
7. femininity
8. virility
9. vitality (bodily or mental)
10. bodily ease (*sukha*)
11. " pain (*dukkha*)
12. gladness (*somanassa*)
13. sadness (*domanassa*)
14. indifference (*upekkhā*)
15. faith (*saddhā*)
16. energy (*viriya*)
17. mindfulness (*sati*)
18. concentration (*samādhi*)
19. wisdom (*paññā*)
20. the thought: "I shall come to know the yet unknown" (*an-aññātaññassāmi t'indriya*)
21. perfect wisdom, or "gnosis" (*aññā*)

22. the faculty of "one with gnosis" (*aññātāv'indriya*)

About the details, see Guide V.

§159 The Six Sense Faculties

SN 48:29

(1–6) There are six faculties, O monks: the eye-faculty, ear-faculty, nose-faculty, tongue-faculty, body-faculty, mind-faculty.

All the monks and brahmins who do not, according to reality, understand the arising and cessation of these six faculties, nor their enjoyment and misery, nor the escape therefrom, all these are among the monks not considered as monks, among the brahmins not considered as brahmins; nor will those venerable ones, already during lifetime, themselves understand the goal of monkhood and brahminhood, nor realize it and make it their own.

All those monks and brahmins, however, who, according to reality, understand the arising and cessation of these six faculties, and their enjoyment and misery, and the escape therefrom, they are all among monks considered as monks, among brahmins considered as brahmins. And all these worthy ones will, already during lifetime, themselves understand the goal of monkhood and brahminhood, realize it, and make it their own.

SN 48:42

(1–5) The five faculties have different fields and different objects, and none of these faculties partakes of the field and object of the other. These faculties are: eye, ear, nose, tongue, and body.

For those five faculties, however, mind forms a support, and mind partakes of their fields and objects.

Three Faculties

SN 48:22

(7–9) There are three faculties, O monks; femininity, virility, and vitality.

§160 The Five Feeling Faculties

SN 48:38

(10–14) There are five faculties (feelings), O monks: (bodily) ease, (bodily) pain, gladness, sadness, and indifference.

Upekkhā (indifference) is here not identical with the lofty and ethical "equanimity," though both are called by the same Pāli name. *Upekkhā,* as indifferent feeling, belongs to the feeling-group, while *upekkhā,* as an ethical quality (equanimity), belongs to the mental formations group.

But what, O monks, is the faculty of bodily ease (*sukh'indriya*)? Whatever is bodily pleasant and agreeable, pleasant and agreeable feeling due to bodily impression, this is called the faculty of bodily ease.

And what, O monks, is the faculty of bodily pain (*dukkh'indriya*)? Whatever is bodily painful and disagreeable, painful and disagreeable feeling due to bodily impression, this is called the faculty of bodily pain.

And what, O monks, is the faculty of gladness (*somanass'indriya*)? Whatever is mentally pleasant and agreeable, mentally pleasant and agreeable feeling due to mental impression, this is called the faculty of gladness.

And what, O monks, is the faculty of sadness (*domanass'indriya*)? Whatever is mentally unpleasant and disagreeable, unpleasant and disagreeable feeling due to mental impression, this is called the faculty of sadness.

And what, O monks, is the faculty of indifference (*upekkh'indriya*)? What there is of bodily or mental feeling neither pleasant nor unpleasant, this is called the faculty of indifference.

Now, what concerns the faculty of bodily ease and the faculty of gladness, they are both to be considered as pleasant feeling (*sukhā vedanā*) And what concerns the faculty of bodily pain and the faculty of sad-mindedness, they are both to be considered as painful feeling (*dukkhā vedanā*). What, however, concerns the faculty of indifference, this is to be considered as neither pleasant nor painful feeling (*adukkham-asukhā vedanā*)

Thus these five faculties, being five, become three; and having become three, they again become five, according to the way of presentation.

SN 48:32

Whenever, O monks, the noble disciple, according to reality, has understood the arising and vanishing of these five faculties (feelings) as well as their enjoyment and misery, and the escape therefrom, then it is said of this noble disciple that he has entered the stream (*sotāpanna*), forever escaped the states of woe, and is assured of final enlightenment.

§161 The Five Spiritual Faculties

SN 48:10

(15–19) There are five (mental) faculties, O monks. They are: faith, energy, mindfulness, concentration, and wisdom.

But what is the faculty of faith (*saddhā*)? Here the noble disciple is filled with faith. He has confidence in the Enlightenment of the Perfect One thus namely: "This Blessed One is truly holy, enlightened, perfect in knowledge and conduct, sublime, the knower of the worlds, the incomparable leader of persons to be trained, the Master of humans and gods, the Enlightened One, the Blessed One." This, O monks, is called the faculty of faith.

But what is the faculty of energy (*viriya*)? Here the noble disciple incites his mind to overcome the unwholesome states and gain the wholesome states, is steadfast, of untiring effort; and with regard to the wholesome states he does not neglect his duties. He incites his will to avoid the arising of evil, unwholesome states not yet arisen ... to overcome the evil, unwholesome states already arisen ... to awaken the wholesome states not yet arisen ... to maintain the wholesome states already arisen, not to let them disappear, but to bring them to growth, to maturity, and to full perfection of development; and he strives, puts forth his energy, strains his mind, and struggles. This, O monks, is called the faculty of energy.

And what is the faculty of mindfulness (*sati*)? Here the noble disciple is endowed with highest mindfulness and prudence. What long ago has been done or spoken, he remembers and recalls it to his mind. With regard to the body he dwells in contemplation of the body, with regard to feelings in contemplation of feelings, with regard to mind in contemplation of mind, with regard to mind-objects in contemplation of mind-objects, full of energy, clearly conscious and mindful, after putting away worldly greed and grief. This, O monks, is called the faculty of mindfulness.

And what is the faculty of concentration (*samādhi*)? Here the noble disciple, based on detachment, gains concentration and one-pointedness of mind. Detached from sensual objects, detached from unwholesome things, he enters into the first *jhāna* ... the second *jhāna* ... the third *jhāna* ... the fourth *jhāna*.... This, O monks, is called the faculty of concentration.

And what is the faculty of wisdom (*paññā?*) Here the noble disciple is wise, endowed with wisdom discerning rise and fall, the noble wisdom, the penetrating wisdom, leading to complete cessation of suffering. And according to reality he knows what is suffering, what is the origin of suffering, what is the cessation of suffering, what is the path that leads to the cessation of suffering.

SN 48:8

By what, O monks, is the faculty of faith to be understood? By the four characteristics of stream-entry.

By what, the faculty of energy? By the four right efforts (see §16 and §50).

By what, the faculty of mindfulness? By the four applications of mindfulness (see §129).

By what, the faculty of concentration? By the four *jhānas*.

By what, the faculty of wisdom? By the Four Noble Truths.

The four characteristics of stream-entry are: unshakable faith in the Enlightened One, the Dhamma, the Community of Noble Disciples, and perfect morality. There are also four other characteristics given in the Sutta Piṭaka, namely: friendship with noble persons, listening to the noble doctrine, wise consideration, and practice in accordance with the doctrine.

§162 Three Supramundane Faculties

SN 48:23

(20–22) There are three supramundane faculties, O monks: the feeling of assurance, "I shall come to know the yet unknown"; the faculty of gnosis; the faculty of one with gnosis. These are the three faculties.

The first of these three supramundane faculties is associated with the supramundane path of stream-entry (see B. Dict.: *ariya-puggala*) and forms the foundation to the attainment of arahatship.

The second faculty, perfect wisdom or gnosis (*aññā*), is associated with the fruit of stream-entry and also with the path and fruit of once-return and non-return and the path of arahatship.

The third faculty, of the one with gnosis, is associated with the fruit of arahatship.

Of the twenty-two faculties, (1–5), (7), (8) are corporeal, (9) is either corporeal or mental, and the rest are mental.

(1–11) are, as such, karmically neutral (*avyākata*), (13) is karmically unwholesome (*akusala*) for its being associated with hateful consciousness, (12) may be karmically wholesome, unwholesome, or neutral. For details see Khandha Table: B. Dict.

§163 The Four Noble Truths

SN 56:1

Develop mental concentration, O monks! For the monk who is mentally concentrated sees things according to reality. And what are these things?

"This is suffering," thus he understands according to reality.

"This is the origin of suffering," thus he understands according to reality.

"This is the cessation of suffering," thus he understands according to reality.

"This is the path leading to the cessation of suffering," thus he understands according to reality.

Comprehension and Penetration

According to Vism XVI,84, the knowledge of the four truths is of two kinds:

(1) mundane knowledge, consisting in comprehension (anubodha);

(2) supramundane knowledge, consisting in penetration (paṭivedha).

The penetrating knowledge is associated with the consciousness of the four stages of awakening. It penetrates in one and the same moment simultaneously all the four truths. As it is said:

SN 56:30

Whoever, O monks, understands suffering, understands (at the same moment) also the origin of suffering, the cessation of suffering, and the path leading to the cessation of suffering. And whoever understands the origin of suffering, understands also suffering, the cessation of suffering, and the path leading to the cessation of suffering. And whoever understands the cessation of suffering, understands also suffering, the origin of suffering, and the path leading to the cessation of suffering. And whoever understands the path leading to the cessation of suffering, understands also suffering, the origin of suffering, and the cessation of suffering.

SN 56:29

The noble truth of suffering must be fully comprehended (*pariññeyya*); the noble truth of the origin of suffering must be overcome (*pahātabba*); the noble truth of the cessation of suffering must be realized (*sacchikātabba*); the noble truth of the path leading to the cessation of suffering must be developed (*bhāvetabba*).

In Vism XVI,85, it is said: "Of the four kinds of mundane comprehension, the comprehension of suffering dispels the personality view which is due to one's being steeped in prejudice, the comprehension of the origin of suffering dispels the view of self-annihilation (at death), the comprehension of the cessation of suffering dispels the view of eternalism, the comprehension of the path dispels the view of inefficacy of action." see B. Dict. *diṭṭhi.*

"One must regard suffering as a disease, the origin of suffering as the cause of the disease, the cessation of suffering as the cure of the disease, the path as the medicine" (Vism XVI,87).

"In the highest sense all the four truths are to be regarded as empty, for the reason that there is (1) no sufferer, (2) no doer, (3) no liberated one, (4) no pursuer of the path. Therefore it is said:

"Mere suffering exists, no sufferer is found.
The deed is, but no doer of the deed is there.
Nibbāna is, but not the man that enters it.
The path is, but no traveller on it is seen.

"Of permanence, bliss, personality, and beauty
Are empty both the first and second truths,
Void of an ego is the deathless realm;
And the path is void of bliss, ego, and permanence."

(Vism XVI,90)

§164 The First Truth

The first noble truth is not limited to actual suffering as feeling, but it teaches that, in consequence of the universal sway of impermanence over all phenomena of existence, even the highest states of bliss are subject to change and dissolution, hence miserable and unsatisfactory, and that everything in existence carries the germ of suffering. Cf. Yam. (Guide VI, v.)

SN 56:13

What now, O monks, is the noble truth of suffering? The proper answer would be: The five groups of existence that form the objects of clinging (*upādāna-kkhandha*), that is to say: the corporeality group, the feeling group, the perception group, the mental formations group, the consciousness group (see §146).

§ 165 The Second and Third Truths

MN 28

Whoever sees dependent origination, sees the Dhamma; and whoever sees the Dhamma, sees dependent origination (see §168ff.). Now, dependently originated are the five groups forming the objects of clinging. Thus, whatever there exists of sensual desire, clinging, inclination, and enchantment with regard to these five groups, this is called the origin of suffering. Whatever there exists of detachment, and of overcoming of craving and desire with regard to these five groups, this is called the cessation of suffering.

SN 12:17

Whoever, Kassapa, says that the doer (of a deed) and the receiver of the karmic result are one and the same person, and thus teaches that suffering has been produced by the being himself that has existed from the very beginning, such a one is seized by the eternity view (*sassata-diṭṭhi*).

Whoever says that the doer and the receiver are two different persons, and thus teaches that the suffering by which the one being is overwhelmed is produced by the other being, such a one is seized by the annihilation view (*uccheda-diṭṭhi*).

These two extremes, however, the Blessed One has avoided and shown the truth (of non-self and conditionality) that keeps in the middle between the two, namely: Thus, conditioned by ignorance are the karma-formations; by the karma-formations, consciousness; by consciousness, mind and corporeality; by mind and corporeality, the six bases; by the six bases, impression; by impression, feeling;

by feeling, craving; by craving, clinging; by clinging, (the karma-process and rebirth-process of) becoming;—by (the karma-process of) becoming, rebirth; by rebirth, old age and death, sorrow, lamentation, pain, grief, and despair. Thus arises this whole mass of suffering.

What, O monks, is the cessation of suffering? Through the complete overcoming and cessation of ignorance there comes about the cessation of karma-formations; through the cessation of karma-formations the cessation of consciousness (after death); through the cessation of consciousness, the cessation of mind and corporeality; through the cessation of mind and corporeality, the cessation of the six base; through the cessation of the six bases; the cessation of impression; through the cessation of impression; the cessation of feeling; through the cessation of feeling, the cessation of craving; through the cessation of craving, the cessation of clinging; through the cessation of clinging, the cessation of (the karma-process and rebirth-process of) becoming; through the cessation of (the karma-process of) becoming; the cessation of rebirth; through the cessation of rebirth comes about the cessation of old age and death, sorrow, lamentation, pain, grief, and despair. Thus comes about the cessation of this whole mass of suffering.

§ 166 The Fourth Truth

MN 117 distinguishes a mundane (*lokiya*) and a supramundane (*lokuttara)* Eightfold Path. The latter is present only in the moment of path or fruit of the four stages of awakening.

MN 117

What, O monks, is the noble right concentration (*ariya-sammāsamādhi*) with its foundation and its equipment? There is right understanding, right thought, right speech, right bodily action, right livelihood, right effort, and right mindfulness; and the one-pointedness of mind (*citt'ekaggatā*) endowed with these seven links of the path, this is called right concentration with its foundation and its equipment.

I tell you, O monks: right understanding is of two kinds. The understanding that alms and offerings are not useless; that there is fruit and result of good and bad actions; that there are such things as this life and the next life, etc.: this is called the mundane right understanding which yields worldly fruits and brings good results.

But whatever there is of wisdom and penetration, of right understanding, conjoined with the path (of stream-entry, etc.), the mind being turned away from the world and conjoined with the path, the holy path being pursued: this is called the supramundane right understanding (*lokuttara-sammādiṭṭhi*), which is free from bias, is not of this world, but is supramundane and conjoined with the path.

Now, in understanding wrong understanding as wrong, and right understanding as right, one practises right understanding; and in making effort to overcome wrong understanding and to arouse right understanding, one practises right effort; and in overcoming wrong understanding with attentive mind, and dwelling with attentive mind in the possession of right understanding, one practises right mindfulness. Hence, there are three things that accompany and follow upon right understanding, namely: right understanding, right effort, and right mindfulness.

Now, in understanding wrong thought as wrong, and right thought as right, one practises right understanding ... right speech ... right bodily action ... right livelihood; and in making effort to overcome wrong livelihood and to arouse right livelihood, one practises right effort; and in overcoming wrong livelihood with attentive mind and dwelling with attentive mind in the possession of right livelihood, one practises right mindfulness. Hence, there are three things that accompany and follow upon right livelihood, namely: right understanding, right effort, and right mindfulness.

§167 The Dawn of Understanding

SN 56:37

Just, O monks, as the dawn is the forerunner of the rising sun and its first indication, just so, is the penetration of the Four Noble Truths, according to reality, preceded by right understanding; and right understanding is its first indication. For, of one who is filled with right understanding, one may expect that he will, according to reality, understand what is suffering, what is the origin of suffering, what is the cessation of suffering, and what is the path leading to the cessation of suffering.

About the true nature of the Noble Eightfold Path the reader is referred to B. Dict. *magga.*

§168 Dependent Origination

(*paṭicca-samuppāda*)

Whatever has been said by Western authors about this extraordinarily important doctrine is nothing but a mere groping about in the dark (see App. to Guide). The author's first short treatise on this subject which still, today, proves correct, appeared as a footnote in his translation of AN III 61 (1923). Thereafter followed an essay, based on Vism XVII, Paṭṭh, and Comy. in which the twenty-four modes of conditions are applied. It appeared in Singapore (1933), Calcutta (Maha Bodhi Journal, 1934), Kandy (1937), and as App. to the Guide (Colombo 1938). After that appeared the more or less popular lecture on *paṭicca-samuppāda,* held at the Ceylon University, Colombo 1938 (reprinted in Fund.). A short treatise is found in B. Dict. For a detailed explanation of all the twenty-four modes of conditionality, see B. Dict. *paccaya.*

The most important Suttas about this subject are found in DN 15; SN II; and MN 9, 38. For a clear survey of the whole, see the chart on the following page.

§169 SN 12:2

I will show you and explain to you, O monks, dependent origination. Therefore listen and pay heed to my words.

What now, O monks, is dependent origination? Thus, conditioned by ignorance are the karma-formations; by the karma-formations, consciousness; by consciousness, mind and corporeality; by mind and corporeality, the six bases; by the six bases, impression; by impression, feeling; by feeling, craving; by craving, clinging; by clinging, (the karma-process and rebirth-process of) becoming; by (the karma-process of) becoming, rebirth; by rebirth, old age and death, sorrow, lamentation, pain, grief, and despair. Thus arises this whole mass of suffering.

But what, O monks, is rebirth (11)? The birth of beings belonging to this or that order of beings, their being born, their conception and springing into existence, the manifestation of the groups of existence, arising of sense activity: this is called rebirth.

By birth is here meant the entire embryonic process, beginning with conception and ending with parturition.

But what, O monks, are the six bases (5)? Eye, ear, nose, tongue, body, and mind-base: these are called the six bases.

But what, O monks, is mind and corporeality (*nāma-rūpa)*? Feeling, perception, volition, impression (sensual or mental), advertence (*vedanā, saññā, cetanā, phassa, manasikāra*): these are called mind. The four primary elements (solid, liquid, heat, motion); and corporeality depending on them: these are called corporeality. Thus there is mind, and there is corporeality: these are called mind and corporeality.

In other places, as a rule, all the four mental groups (*nāma-kkhanda*) are called mind (*nāma*). At times they are divided into consciousness (*citta*) and mental factors (*cetasika*: feeling, perception, and fifty formations. For those karma-resultant mental states, however, with which we are here concerned, only the above mentioned five mental factors "inseparably associated with all consciousness" (*sabba-citta-sādhāraṇa*) come into consideration. The Abhidhamma (Dhs) adds another two constant mental factors: concentration and mental vitality.

But what, O monks, are the karma-formations (*saṅkhārā*)? There are three karma-formations: (wholesome and unwholesome) karma-formations in deed, word, and thought: these are called the karma-formations.

This explanation is found again and again in the Suttas. One often finds also the division into meritorious (*puñña*), demeritorious (*apuñña*), and imperturbable (*āneñja*) karma-formations, of which the latter belong to the immaterial sphere (see §119ff.). In all cases wholesome and unwholesome volitional actions (*kamma*) are meant.

§170 SN 12:51

(1) If, O monks, a man filled with *ignorance* (*avijjā*) performs a meritorious karma-formation (*saṅkhārā*), then consciousness (*viññāṇa*) brings him merit. If he performs a demeritorious karma-formation, then consciousness brings him demerit. If he performs an imperturbable karma-formation, then consciousness brings imperturbability.

If, however, in the monk ignorance has disappeared and wisdom arisen, then, through cessation of ignorance and the arising of wisdom, he no longer performs any meritorious, demeritorious, or imperturbable karma-formations. But, while performing no more karma and producing no more volitional activity (*cetanā*), he no longer clings to anything in the world. While no more clinging to anything, he trembles no more. While trembling no more, he attains in his inner heart Nibbāna. And he knows: "Rebirth has ceased, the holy life is fulfilled, the task is done, and nothing further remains after this."

(1–2) What do you think, O monks: Could the man in whom the taints (*āsava*; and *ignorance*) have vanished, still perform meritorious karma-formations, etc.?

"No, O Venerable One."

(2–3) But if there are no more *karma-formations* could there, after the cessation of all the karma-formations, still arise *consciousness* (in a new mother's womb after death)?

"No, O Venerable One."

(3–4) But if *consciousness* no more exists, can there, in absence of consciousness, arise *mind-and-corporeality* (*nāma-rūpa*)?

"No, O Venerable One."

This passage is apparently to be read thus: *Sabbaso vā pana viññāṇe asati viññāṇa-nirodhā nāma-rūpaṃ paññāyethāti?*

§171 DN 15

(3–4) "Conditioned by consciousness is mind-and-corporeality," thus it is said. This, however, is to be understood in the following way: If consciousness, Ananda, were not to enter the mother's womb, would there arise mind-and-corporeality (i.e. the foetus) in the mother's womb?

"No, O Venerable One."

Thus, Ānanda, consciousness is the cause and reason, the origin and condition of mind-and-corporeality.

§172 MN 9

(1) But what, O brothers, is ignorance (*avijjā*)? What is its origin? What is its cessation? What is the path leading to its cessation?

Not to understand suffering, its origin, its cessation, and the path leading to its cessation: this is called ignorance. Through the arising of taints (sensual taint, taint of existence, taint of ignorance) there comes about the arising of ignorance, through cessation of the taints the cessation of ignorance; and this Noble Eightfold Path is the path leading to the cessation of taints, namely: right understanding, right thought, right speech, right bodily action, right livelihood, right effort, right mindfulness, and right concentration.

Just as the arising of all the other mental phenomena is conditioned, exactly so it is with the arising of ignorance. Thus ignorance is not the causeless primal cause of existence, says Vism XVII,36, but forms only the starting point in the formula of dependent origination. In AN 20:61 it is said: "There is not to be found, O monks, a first beginning of ignorance, before which there was no ignorance and only after which, ignorance has arisen. Thus it is said, O monks, ignorance is known as something conditionally arisen."

§173 MN 57

Suppose, Puṇṇa, someone performs painful karma-formations in bodily deed, word, and thought. Having performed painful karma-formations, he descends to a painful world. Having descended to a painful world, painful impressions attack him, such as the beings in hell. Thus, Puṇṇa, it happens each time with the rebirth of beings: According to one's actions (karma) one will be reborn; and having been reborn, the impressions fall upon him. Therefore, Puṇṇa, I say: "Beings are heirs of their actions."

From the Suttas quoted above, we have clearly and unambiguously seen that by the second link of the formula, karma-formations (*saṅkhārā*), is meant wholesome and unwholesome karma, or action, i.e. volitional activities (*cetanā*) by body, speech, and mind; and that by the third link, consciousness (*viññāṇa*), is meant karma-produced consciousness serving here as the representative of future life, and appearing for the first time at conception in the mother's womb.

Simultaneously with consciousness, however—at conception as well as during life—there arise those few karma-resultant mental factors inseparably bound up with all consciousness, namely: feeling, perception, volition, etc. (explained above) as "mind" (*nāma*). Just so the corporeality of the new embryonic being arises simultaneously with conception, conditioned by it. These mental and corporeal (*nāma-rūpa*) groups are therefore conditioned by the simultaneously arising rebirth-consciousness (*paṭisandhi-viññāṇa*). Thus at conception the third link, consciousness, and the fourth link, mind-and-corporeality, are conditions to each other by way of conascence or simultaneity (*saha-jāta*), mutuality (*añña-mañña*), association, etc. Therefore it is repeatedly said in the Suttas that mind and corporeality are also a condition for consciousness (*nāma-rūpa-paccayā viññāṇaṃ*).

That *bhava* (here *kamma-bhava*, karma-process) in the tenth proposition ("Through the process of becoming rebirth is conditioned") must belong to the present existence, and rebirth (*jāti*) to the future one, follows clearly from the above Suttas.

The Abhidhamma divides the process of becoming into (1) the active or karma-process (*kamma-bhava*: 1, 2, 8, 9, 10); and (2) the karma-resultant passive rebirth-process (*uppatti-bhava*: 3–7; identical with 11–12). Hence the tenth proposition says, in other words, that rebirth is conditioned by karma.

§174 AN 3:61

Now, what is called the noble truth of the cessation of suffering?

Through the complete overcoming and cessation of ignorance there comes about the cessation of karma-formations; through the cessation of karma-formations the cessation of consciousness (after death); through the cessation of consciousness, the cessation of mind and corporeality; through the cessation of mind and corporeality; the cessation of the six bases, through the cessation of the six bases; the cessation of impression, through the cessation of impression; the cessation of feeling; through the cessation of feeling; the cessation of craving; through the cessation of craving; the cessation of clinging; through the cessation of clinging, the cessation of (the karma-process and rebirth-process of) becoming; through the cessation of(the karma-process process of) becoming, the cessation of rebirth; through the cessation of rebirth comes about the cessation of old age, death, sorrow, lamentation, pain, grief, and despair. Thus comes about the cessation of this whole mass of suffering.

§175 **III. Purity of understanding**
(*diṭṭhi-visuddhi*)

The first two kinds of purity, i.e. purity of morality and of mind, have already been treated in the first and second section of this book, under the headings of (A) Morality and (B) Concentration.

About the third purity, purity of understanding, it is said at Vism XVIII,37: "What is called 'purity of understanding' is the understanding, according to reality, of mental and corporeal phenomena (*nāma-rūpa*) which, while determining in many ways the mental and corporeal, has abandoned the belief in personality, and has thus taken root in the soil of non-delusion."

In other words, the third purity is attained by way of a thorough analysis of mind and body, and by the subsequent insight that these mental and material phenomena are void of a self. That analysis may make use of those three divisions into groups of existence, bases, and elements, which form the first three objects of insight-wisdom, dealt with, in detail, in the preceding paragaraphs of this section (§§145–57). The understanding of non-self resulting from that analysis, may be illustrated by the following texts.

SN 5:10

When certain things we find combined
We speak of chariot, speak of car.
Just so when these five groups appear,
We use the designation "being."

Vism XIX,20

No doer of the deeds is found,
No being that may reap their fruits;
Empty phenomena roll on;
This is the only right view.

No god nor Brahmā can be called
The maker of this wheel of life;
Empty phenomena roll on,
Dependent on conditions all.

The groups of life become dissolved,
There is no being to be found;
The dissolution of the groups
Is what most people would call death.

It 49

Fettered by two views, O monks, some among the heavenly beings and humans adhere, others overshoot the mark; and only those that have eyes can see.

But how, O monk, do some adhere? Heavenly beings and humans are delighted in existence, enraptured in existence, gladdened by existence. Though one may teach them the doctrine about the cessation of existence, their mind does not drive forward to it, is not delighted in it, does not become fixed in it, does not incline towards it. Thus, O monks, do some adhere.

But how, O monks, do some overshoot the mark? Some who are disgusted with existence, feeling aversion for it and detesting it, praise non-existence on the grounds that this very self, after the dissolution of the body, becomes destroyed and annihilated, and no longer continues after death. Thus, O monks, do some overshoot the mark.

But how is it, O monks, that only those who have eyes can see? Here the monk sees the existent as existent, and the non-existent as non-existent. Thus, O monks, only those who have eyes can see.

§176 The Three Characteristics of Existence

MN 147

What do you think, Rāhula: Is the eye permanent or impermanent?

"Impermanent, Venerable One."

But what is impermanent, is this pleasant or painful?

"Painful, Venerable One."

But of that which is impermanent, painful, and subject to change, can it be rightly said: "That belongs to me, that I am, that is my self?"

"No, Venerable One."

What do you think, Rāhula: Are visible forms ... eye-consciousness ... visual impression ... feeling due to visual impression ... perception ... mental formations ... consciousness, etc., permanent or impermanent?

"Impermanent, Venerable One."

But, what is impermanent, is this pleasant or painful?

"Painful, Venerable One."

But of that which is impermanent, painful, and subject to change, can it be rightly said: "That belongs to me, that I am, that is my self?"

"No, Venerable One." ...

Understanding thus, Rāhula, the noble disciple turns away from the eye, ear, nose, tongue, body, mind, mind-consciousness—from whatsoever feeling, perception, mental formations, and consciousness arise conditioned by impression. And while turning away from them, he becomes detached. And through detachment he is liberated. And in the Liberated One there arises the knowledge, "I am liberated." And he understands: "Rebirth has ceased, the holy life is fulfilled, the task is done, and nothing further remains after this."

§177 Non-Self

SN 35:90

One should not imagine oneself to be identical with the eye, or contained in it, or independent of it, or the owner of it. One should not imagine oneself to be identical with the ear, nose, tongue, body, mind, or with mind-object, mind-consciousness, mind-impression, with the agreeable, disagreeable, and indifferent feeling due to mind-impression; one should not imagine oneself to be contained in it, or independent of it, or the owner of it.

One should not imagine oneself to be identical with the whole world, or contained in it, or independent it, or the owner of it....

Thus, free from imagining, one clings no more to anything in the world. Clinging no more, one is no more agitated. Being no more agitated, one reaches in one's own person the cessation of all vanity (Nibbāna), and one understands: "Rebirth has ceased, the holy life is fulfilled, the task is done, and nothing further remains after this."

> In accordance with the beginning of this Sutta, one has to understand the beginning of MN 1: "He imagines himself to be identical with the earth, or contained in it, or independent of it, or the owner of it, etc." Neumann, Silācāra, and Chalmers did not notice that the text refers to personality-view and went quite astray in their translations.

The Early Masters (cited at Vism XVIII,31)

> In truth there is only this body and this mind,
> And there cannot be found a being or person,
> Quite empty is this compound like a swivel-doll,
> A heap of misery resembling wood and straw.

§178 Emptiness

SN 35:85

" 'Empty is the world! Empty is the world!': thus it is said, Venerable One. But why, Venerable One, is the world called empty?"

Because, Ānanda, the world is empty of a self and of anything belonging to a self, therefore the world is called empty.

Empty, indeed, of a self or of something belonging to a self are eye, visible form, eye-consciousness, etc. Thus, Ānanda, because all things are empty of a self and of anything belonging to a self, the world is called empty.

§179 Perfection of the Path

MN 149

Here, O monks, someone knows and understands according to reality the eye, visible object, eye-consciousness, eye-impression, and the agreeable, disagreeable, and indifferent feeling due to eye-impression; but he does not cling to it. He knows and understands according to reality the ear ... nose ... tongue ... body ... mind, mind-object, mind-consciousness, mind-impression, and the agreeable, disagreeable, and indifferent feeling due to mind-impression; but he does not cling to it; and dwelling unfettered, undeluded, in the contemplation of misery, there comes about the breakup of the five groups forming the objects of clinging; and the craving which, leading to ever new rebirth and accompanied by lust and greed, now here and now there finds ever fresh delight, this craving vanishes. Also the vexation, torment, and agitation of mind and of mental factors come to disappear. And he experiences happiness of mind and of mental factors.

(1) Now, what there is of understanding in such a one, that counts as right understanding. (2) What there is of thinking in him, that counts as right thought. (6) What there is of effort in him, that counts as right effort. (7) What there is of mindfulness in him, that counts as right mindfulness. (8) What there is of concentration in him, that counts as right concentration. But already previously his bodily action, speech, and livelihood (3–5) were purified. In this way the Noble Eightfold Path reaches full development in him.

While he is developing this Noble Eightfold Path, the four applications of mindfulness reach full development, as well as the four right efforts, the four roads to power, the five mental faculties, the five mental powers, and the seven factors of enlightenment.

> About these terms see B. Dict.: *satipaṭṭhāna, sammappadhāna, iddhipāda, indriya, bala, bojjhaṅga.*

Two things, further are in him linked as a pair, namely tranquillity (*samatha*) and insight (*vipassanā*; see B. Dict.). (1) And those things that are to be wisely comprehended, he wisely comprehends. (2) Those things that are to be wisely overcome, he wisely overcomes. (3) Those things that are to be wisely realized, he wisely realizes. (4) Those things that are to be wisely developed, he wisely develops.

(1) But which things, O monks, are to be wisely comprehended? The answer is: The five groups forming the objects of clinging, namely: the corporeality group, the feeling group, the perception group, the mental formations group, the consciousness group. These things are to be wisely comprehended.

(2) But which things, O monks, are to be wisely overcome? Ignorance (*avijjā*) and craving for existence (*bhava-taṇhā*): these things are to be wisely overcome.

(3) But which things, O monks, are to be wisely realized? Wisdom (*vijjā*) and deliverance (*vimutti*): these things are to be wisely realized.

(4) But which things, O monks, are to be wisely developed? Tranquillity (*samatha*) and insight (*vipassanā*): these things are to be wisely developed.

§180 **IV. Purity of Escape from doubt**

(*kaṅkhā-vitaraṇa-visuddhi*)

"Purity of escape from doubt" is that knowledge which comes about by comprehending the conditions for the arising of the mental and physical phenomena (*nāmarūpa*) and which is free from all the doubts with regard to the three times. The understanding of dependent origination and of karma and rebirth are therefore also included here.

Pṭs II, 63–64

Whoever considers all things as impermanent (*anicca*), he sees and understands the conditions for existence (*nimitta*) according to reality. Therefore one speaks of right understanding. Once all formations have been well understood by him as impermanent, his doubts will disappear.

Whoever considers all things as painful (*dukkha*), he sees and understands continuity of existence (*pavatta*) according to reality. Therefore one speaks of right understanding.

Once all formations have been well understood by him as painful, his doubts will disappear.

Whoever considers all things as non-self (*anattā*), he sees and understands the continuity of existence according to reality. Therefore one speaks of right understanding. Once all things have been well understood by him as non-self, his doubts will disappear.

Now, what here is called "understanding according to reality," "right understanding," and "escape from doubt," these three terms have all one and the same meaning, and they are different only in name.

§181 Ud 5:7

Thus have I heard. Once the Blessed One dwelt in the Jeta Grove near Sāvatthī, in the monastery of Anāthapiṇḍika. On that occasion the Venerable Revata the Doubter sat not far from the Blessed One, cross-legged, with body erect, and pondered on his own purity of escape from doubt. Then the Blessed One noticed him as he was sitting there and pondering on his own purity of escape from doubt. Noticing this fact, the Blessed One on that occasion made the solemn utterance:

Whatever kinds of doubts may arise,
Be it on this world, or the world to come,
All these the steadfast monk has overcome,
The strenuous one, who loves the holy life.

§182 MN 2

While the ignorant worldling ... considers things unworthy of consideration and does not consider things worthy of consideration, there arise in him unarisen taints, and the already arisen taints grow stronger. And unwisely he considers thus: "Have I been in the past? Or have I not been in the past? What have I been in the past? How have I been in the past? From what state into what state did I change in the past? Shall I be in the future? Or shall I not be in the future? What shall I be in the future? How shall I be in the future? From what state into what state shall I change in the future?" And also the present fills him with doubt: "Am I? Or am I not? What am I? How am I? This being, whence has it come? Whither will it go?"

The learned, noble disciple, however, ... considers things worthy of consideration and does not consider things unworthy of consideration. He wisely considers what suffering is. He wisely considers what the origin of suffering is. He wisely considers what the cessation of suffering is. He wisely considers what the path is that leads to the cessation of suffering. And by thus considering, three fetters vanish in him: personality view, scepticism, and clinging to rule and ritual (*sakkāya-diṭṭhi, vicikicchā, sīlabbata-parāmāsa).*

> The wise person, who has escaped from all the aforementioned sixteen doubts, sees in reality only mental and corporeal phenomena kept going through the concatenation of karmic causes and results. And he does not see any "doer" besides the deed, nor any "receiver" of the karma-result beside the result, nor any self within or without the phenomena. And he knows that it is only by way of conventional language that one may speak of a "doer" or a "receiver" of karma-result. Thus was it said by the Early Masters (Vism XIX,20):
>
> No doer of the deeds is found,
> No being that may reap their fruits;
> Empty phenomena roll on:
> This is the only right view.
>
> Pṭs II,62
>
> Who wishes to escape from doubt,
> Should be attentive and alert,
> And should of mind and body both
> Perceive the cause and origin.

§183 **Karma and Rebirth**

SN 35:145

I shall show and explain to you, O monks, old karma and new karma, as well as the the cessation of karma, and the path leading to its cessation.

But what, O monks, is old karma (correctly speaking, the result of the old karma or action)? Eye, ear, nose, tongue, body, and mind, are to be considered as (the result of) old karma, i.e. as karma-born (*kammaja*), produced by karma-volition, and as endowed with sensibility. This, O monks, is called old karma.

But what, O monks, is new karma? Whatever karma, O monks, is presently performed in bodily deed, word, and thought. This is called new karma.

But what, O monks, is the cessation of karma? That one, through the cessation of karma in bodily deed, word, and thought, attains deliverance: this is called the cessation of karma.

And what, O monks, is the path leading to the cessation of karma? It is this Noble Eightfold Path, consisting in right understanding, right thought, right speech, right action, right livelihood, right effort, right mindfulness, and right concentration. This is called the path leading to the cessation of karma.

§184 AN 4:171

If, O monks, there is this body, then through volition manifested in bodily deeds (*kāya-sañcetanā*) there arises pleasure or pain. If there is speech, then through volition manifested in words (*vacī-sañcetanā*) there arises pleasure or pain. If there is mind, then through volition manifested in thoughts (*mano-sañcetanā*) there arises pleasure or pain.

Due to ignorance (*avijjā*), O monks, one performs either through one's own impulse (*sāmaṃ*) a karma-formation (*saṅkhāra*) by body, speech, or mind, whereby pleasure or pain arises to oneself; or one is induced to it by others.

Clearly knowing, O monks, one performs this karma-formation, or not clearly knowing one performs this karma-formation, whereby weal or woe arises to oneself.

It seems probable that the Dhammasaṅgaṇī, the first book of the Abhidhamma Piṭaka, has drawn on this text as the basis for its division of the classes of karmically wholesome and unwholesome consciousness into spontaneous or "unprepared" classes (*a-saṅkhārika*) and stimulated or "prepared" classes (*sa-saṅkhārika*); again, into such classes that are associated with either "knowledge" or "wrong views" (*ñāṇa-* or *diṭṭhi-sampayutta*), and in such as are not associated therewith. Cp. Guide I and Table.

In all those things, O monks, ignorance is the leader. After the complete fading away and cessation of ignorance, however, there is no more that body, speech, and mind, conditioned through which pleasure or pain might arise to oneself. No more fertile ground is there, no more foundation, no more base, no more cause, conditioned through which pleasure or pain might arise to oneself.

§185 AN 6:63

Karma, O monks, should be known, as well as its dependent origination, its varieties, its result, its cessation, and the path leading to its cessation....

But what, O monks, is karma? It is volition (*cetanā*) that I call karma or action, for through volition one performs action by body, speech, or mind. This is called karma.

But what is the dependent origination of karma? The dependent origination of karma is by sense-impression (*phassa*).

But what are the varieties of karma? There is karma that ripens in hell, karma that ripens in the animal kingdom, karma that ripens in the realm of ghosts, karma that ripens in the human world, karma that ripens in the world of heavenly beings. These are called the varieties of karma.

But what is the result of karma? There is a threefold result of karma, I say: either during this life, or in the next birth, or at later times. This is called the result of karma.

But what is the cessation of karma? By the cessation of sense-impression comes the cessation of karma. And this Noble Eightfold Path is the path leading to the cessation of karma, namely: right understanding, right thought, right speech, right action, right livelihood, right effort, right mindfulness, and right concentration.

§186 About the absence of any ego or self in the process of karma and rebirth, Vism XIX,22 says:

"Comprehending the dependent nature of the mental and corporeal combination (*nāma-rūpa*) by way of the round of karma (ignorance, karma-formation, craving, clinging, and karma-process) and the round of karma-results (consciousness, mind and corporeality, six bases, sense-impression, feeling), he who is freed from doubt with regard to the three times understands all the past, present, and future things with regard to death and rebirth.... He knows: 'The karma-produced groups of the past have ceased in the past. Conditioned, however, through the past karma, other groups have arisen in the present existence; but nothing has passed over from the past to the present existence. Also the karma-produced groups of this existence will become extinguished and nothing will pass over from this existence to the future existence....'

"Just as the flame of a light does not pass over from one wick to another, but still the new light arises conditioned through the other flame; just so nothing passes over from the past life to the present life, nor likewise from this to the next life; but conditioned through the groups, bases, and elements of the past life, an arising of these things in the present life takes place: and conditioned through the groups, etc., of the present life, these things arise in the future life."

About the rebirth-process and the subconscious lifestream underlying all existence and karma, see Fund. II.

§187

V. Purity of knowledge and vision regarding path and not-path

(*maggāmagga-ñāṇadassana-visuddhi*)

"By this stage of purity is meant that knowledge which consists in recognizing the right and wrong path: 'This is the path! That is not the path!' " (Vism XX,1).

According to Vism, one who develops insight (*vipassanā*) in order to gain this knowledge should ponder over the characteristics of all forms of existence, and their dependent origination, somewhat after this manner:

SN 22:21

Corporeality is impermanent, produced, of dependent origin, subject to destruction and cessation. Feeling is impermanent ... Perception is impermanent ... Mental formations are impermanent ... Consciousness is impermanent, produced, of dependent origin, subject to destruction and cessation.

SN 22:18–20

Corporeality is impermanent (*anicca*), and also the causes and conditions of its arising are impermanent. How could corporeality, which has arisen out of something impermanent, ever be permanent? Feeling is impermanent .... Perception is impermanent .... Mental formations are impermanent .... Consciousness is impermanent, and also the causes and conditions of its arising are impermanent. How could consciousness, which has arisen out of something impermanent, ever be pleasant?

Corporeality, feeling, perception, mental formations, and consciousness are painful (*dukkha*), and also the causes and conditions of their arising are painful. How could these things, which have arisen out of something painful, ever be happiness?

Corporeality, feeling, perception, mental formations, and consciousness are non-self (*anattā*), and also the causes and conditions of their arising are non-self. How could these things, which have arisen out of something non-self, ever be a self?

Dhp 373–74

The monk in deepest solitude,
Grown still and tranquil in his heart,
Feels superhuman happiness,
While clearly he perceives the truth.

Whenever he reflects upon
The rise and passing of the groups,
He's filled with rapture and with bliss,
While he beholds the Deathless Realm.

§188 Rapture (*pīti*) is one of the ten mental phenomena which arise during insight exercises, and which to the beginner may become a "defilement of insight" (*vipassan' ūpakkilesa*), making him believe that he has attained the right path or even the goal. They are: a luminous aura, knowledge, rapture, tranquillity, joy, determination, energy, awareness, equanimity, delight. The experienced disciple, however, understands all these things as impermanent, suffering, and non-self, and knows that they are not the path, but that only insight (*vipassanā*) is to be considered the right path.

§189 About the impermanence and suffering of all forms of existence, it is said in Vism XX,72:

All life and all existence here,
With all its joys and all its woe,
Rests on a single state of mind,
And quick passes that moment by.

Nay, even gods, whose life does last
For eighty-four thousand kalpas,
Do not remain one and the same,
Not even for two single thoughts.

Those groups that passed away just now,
Those groups that will pass later on,
Those groups just passing in between,
They're not in nature different.

Not in the future moment does one live,
One now lives in the present moment.
"When consciousness dissolves, the world is dead":
This utterance is true in the highest sense.

No hoarding up of things passed by,
No heaping up in future time!

And things arisen are all like
The mustard seed on pointed awl!

The groups of life that disappeared
At death, as well as during life,
Have all alike become extinct,
And never will they rise again.

Out of the unseen did they rise,
Into the unseen do they pass.
Just as the lightning flashes forth,
So do they flash and pass away.

About the purity of knowledge and vision regarding path and not-path, it is said:

§190 AN 10:26

Some monks and brahmins who consider the attainment of the earth kasina (see §75) as the highest have attained this goal. The highest, however, that can be obtained in the attainment of the earth kasina, this the Blessed One has fully understood. And fully understanding this, the Blessed One has understood its enjoyment, understood its misery, understood the escape from it, understood the knowledge and vision regarding path and not-path, and he beheld the attainment of the goal and the peace of heart.

"Through purity of understanding (*diṭṭhi-visuddhi*) the disciple devoted to the practice has, in comprehending mentality and corporeality (*nāma-rūpa*), determined the truth of suffering. Through purity of escape from doubt (*kaṅkhā-vitaraṇavisuddhi*) he has, in comprehending the conditions, determined the truth of knowledge and vision regarding path and not-path" (Vism XX,130).

§191 VI. Purity of the knowledge and vision of progress

(*paṭipadā-ñāṇadassana-visuddhi*)

By this stage of purity is meant, according to Vism XXI,1, the knowledge resulting from the following nine kinds of insight knowledge, namely:

(1) contemplation of arising and passing (*udayabbayānupassanā*),
(2) contemplation of dissolution (*bhaṅgānupassanā*),
(3) awareness of terror (*bhayatupaṭṭhāna*),
(4) contemplation of misery (*ādīnavānupassanā*),
(5) contemplation of turning away (*nibbidānupassanā*),
(6) desire for deliverance (*muccitukamyatā*),
(7) reflective contemplation (*paṭisaṅkhānupassanā*),
(8) equanimity regarding all formations (*saṅkhār' upekkhā*),
(9) adaptation knowledge (*anuloma-ñāṇa*).

§192 (1) contemplation of arising and passing

AN 4:90

Here, O monks, a monk dwells contemplating the arising and passing away of the five groups (forming the objects) of clinging: "Thus is corporeality, thus its arising, thus its passing away; thus is feeling, thus its arising, thus its passing away; thus is perception, thus its arising, thus its passing away; thus are the mental formations, thus their arising, thus their passing away; thus is consciousness, thus its arising, thus its passing away."

§193 (2) contemplation of dissolution

Dhp 170

Just as if he saw a bubble,
Just as if he saw a phantom:
He who thus beholds existence
May elude the eyes of Māra.

The Early Masters

(cited at Vism XXI,24)

The living groups do pass away,
No being is there to be found,
The dissolution of the groups,
Is what the people would call "death."

The man who strives with earnest mind,
Does penetrate the passing groups,

As with a diamond one may cut
A precious stone however hard.

§194

(3) Awareness of terror

Pṭs II,63

To one who considers all formations as impermanent, the conditions (*nimitta*) of existence appear as terror. To one who considers them as suffering, the continuity of existence appears as terror. To one who considers them as non-self, both conditions and continuity appear as terror.

"Conditions of existence" are the past, present, and future karma-formations. "Continuity of existence" is the continuity of corporeal and incorporeal groups of existence.

§195

(4) Contemplation of misery

Pṭs I,59

But how may the "knowledge consisting in awareness of terror" be considered as the "knowledge of misery"?

"The conditions of existence are a terror!": such knowledge consisting in awareness of terror is considered as the knowledge of misery. "The continuity is a terror!" ... "The continuity of existence is a terror!" ... "Conception is a terror!" ... "The course of existence is a terror!" ... "The entering into existence is a terror!" ... "Birth is a terror!" ... "Old age is a terror!" ... "Disease is a terror!" ... "Sorrow ... lamentation ... despair is a terror!": such knowledge consisting in awareness of terror is considered as knowledge of misery.

"The no-more-arising is safety!" this is considered as knowledge of the abode of peace. "The origin of existence is a terror, but no-more-arising is safety!": this is considered as the knowledge of the abode of peace.... "Despair is a terror, but no-more-despair is safety!": this is considered as the knowledge of the abode of peace.

"The origin of existence is misery!": such knowledge consisting in awareness of terror is considered as the knowledge of misery.... "The no-more-arising is happiness!": this is considered as the knowledge of the abode of peace.

"The origin of existence is something worldly!": such knowledge consisting in awareness of terror is considered as the knowledge of misery .... "The no-more-arising is something unworldly!": this is considered as the knowledge of the abode of peace.... "The arising of existence is something worldly, but the no-more-arising is something unworldly!": this is considered as the knowledge of the abode of peace....

"The conditions of existence consist in the karma-formations!": such knowledge consisting in awareness of terror is considered as the knowledge of misery. "The no-more-arising is Nibbāna!"; this is considered as the knowledge of the abode of peace.

"Painful is arising, painful continuity,
Painful also the condition of existence,
Painful heaping up, and painful being born again":
Knowing this, indeed, is knowing misery.

"No more arising, standstill of existence,
No more condition, no more heaping up again,
No birth more": knowing this as happiness,
Is really knowing the abode of peace.

SN 35:13

That the eye is impermanent, suffering, and subject to change, this is the misery of the eye. That the ear... nose ... tongue ... body ... mind are impermanent, suffering, and subject to change, this is their misery.

That visible form ... sound ... odour ... taste ... bodily impression ... mind-object are impermanent, suffering, and subject to change, this is their misery.

§196 **(5) Contemplation of turning away**

This knowledge has the same meaning as the two preceding ones, and differs only in the wording. Because the one knowledge has understood all formations as terror, therefore the name "awareness of terror" has come into use. Because it has made known the misery of all those formations, therefore the name "contemplation of misery" is used. And because it has arisen through the turning away from all those formations, therefore it is called the "turning away." see Pṭs II,63.

§197 **(6) Desire for deliverance**

While the disciple devoted to the practice turns away from all formations of existence and no longer finds delight in them, his mind no longer clings to any formation and he is filled with only the one desire: to be freed from all forms of existence (see Vism XXI,45–46).

§198 **(7) Reflective contemplation**

In order, however, to gain deliverance from all formations of existence, by means of reflective contemplation he again determines the three characteristics of existence and contemplates on the fourfold emptiness (*suññatā*) (see Vism XXI,47–52).

SN 35:85

Empty is this of a self (*attā*) and of anything belonging to a self (*attaniya*).

MN 106

"I am not anywhere anything to any one, and there belongs not to me anywhere anything in any regard."

The monk has comprehended the fourfold emptiness, for (1) he nowhere sees his own self, (2) he can nowhere discover it as belonging to someone else, (3) he nowhere sees another's self, (4) he can nowhere discover it as belonging to himself in any regard. see Vism XXI,7.

"Corporeality is without pith, unsubstantial, void of an imperishable content; void of permanency-content, of happiness-content, of self-content, empty of anything imperishable, anything eternal, of anything not subject to change. Just so with feeling, perception, mental formations, and consciousness.

"Just as a reed, a water bubble, a mirage, a banana tree, or jugglery, are without pith, without contents and empty: just so are corporeality, feeling, perception, mental formations, consciousness, etc., without pith, without contents, and empty" (Vism XXI,53).

Snp 1119

As empty contemplate this world,
Mogharāja, steadily aware.
With self-illusion rooted out,
You will surely escape from death.
The man who thus beholds the world
The King of Death will find no more.

§199 **(8) Equanimity regarding all formations**

After the monk has thus understood all the formations of existence, he no longer clings to anything and is filled with perfect equanimity regarding all formations. The thoughts of "I" and "mine" can no longer arise in him.

Pṭs, Vism, and the commentaries distinguish three aspects of deliverance, i.e. of the supramundane path of stream-entry, etc., namely: signless deliverance (*animitta-vimokkha*), desireless deliverance (*appaṇihita-vimokkha*), and void deliverance (*suññata-vimokkha*). The reason for this is that the path has as object Nibbāna which is considered as the conditionless, signless, and void.

The same threefold division is made in DN 33 with regard to concentration.

By the "three gates to deliverance" are meant the three contemplations on impermanence, suffering, and non-self.

Pṭs II,36

But what is the void deliverance? Here the monk goes to the forest, the foot of a tree, or an empty abode, and he considers for himself thus: "Empty is this of a self, or of anything belonging to a self." Now, in so far as he feels no inclination, his deliverance is called "void deliverance." In so far as he produces thereby no sign (karma), it is called "signless deliverance." And in so far as he thereby feels no desire, it is called "desireless deliverance."

The "equanimity knowledge" is essentially identical with the "desire for deliverance" and the "reflective contemplation" (6 and 7), which constitute the lowest and middle stages, while the equanimity knowledge is considered the highest stage.

§200 **The Seven Noble Disciples**

The seven kinds of noble disciples are often mentioned in the Suttas, e.g. AN 7:14; DN 28, 33; MN 70, etc., also in Pug §§30–36. The seven names are everywhere given in the same order, from the highest to the lowest one. Detailed explanations of all of them, however, are given only in MN 70 and Pug §30. The explanation of 1–3 is found in AN 9:43–45.

MN 70

There are, O monks, seven individuals found in the world, namely:

1. one liberated in both ways (*ubhatobhāga-vimutta*),
2. one liberated by wisdom (*paññā-vimutta*),
3. the body-witness (*kāya-sakkhī*),
4. one attained to understanding (*diṭṭhi-patta*),
5. one liberated by faith (*saddhā-vimutta*),
6. the truth devotee (*dhammānusārī*),
7. the faith-devotee (*saddhānusāri*).

1\. Now who, O monks, is the one liberated in both ways? Here someone has in his own person reached those peaceful uncorporeal deliverances (the formless absorptions) transcending all corporeality. And, after wisely understanding things, his taints (*āsava*) have been destroyed. Such a one, O monks, is called liberated in both ways.

2\. But who, O monks, is the one liberated by wisdom? Here someone has not, in his own person, reached those peaceful uncorporeal deliverances transcending all corporeality. But, after wisely understanding things, his taints have been destroyed. Such a one, O monks, is called liberated by wisdom.

3. But who, O monks, is a body-witness? Here someone has, in his own person, reached those peaceful uncorporeal deliverances transcending all corporeality. But, after wisely understanding things, only some of his taints have been destroyed. Such a one, O monks is called a body-witness.

> According to AN 9:44, every noble disciple who has reached any of the *jhānas* may, in a certain respect, be considered one of the above three noble disciples; in every respect, however, only after having reached all the *jhānas* and the cessation of consciousness. see §206.

4. But who, O monks, is the one attained to understanding? Here someone has not, in his own person, reached those peaceful uncorporeal deliverances transcending all corporeality; and, after wisely understanding things, only some of his taints have been destroyed. But the teaching made known by the Perfect One he has fully comprehended and penetrated. Such a one, O monks, is called one who has attained to understanding.

5. But who, O monks, is the one liberated by faith. Here someone has not, in his own person, reached those peaceful uncorporeal deliverances transcending all corporeality; and, after wisely understanding things, only some of his taints have been destroyed. But his faith in the Perfect One is firmly established, deeply rooted, and steadfast. Such a one, O monks, is called one liberated by faith.

6. But who, O monks, is a truth-devotee? Here someone has not, in his own person, reached those peaceful uncorporeal deliverances transcending all corporeality; nor, after wisely understanding things, have his taints been destroyed. But the teachings made known by the Perfect One find a certain understanding in him, and he is endowed with such faculties as faith, energy, mindfulness, concentration, and wisdom. Such a one, O monks, is called a truth-devotee.

7. But who, O monks, is a faith-devotee? Here someone has not, in his own person, reached those peaceful

uncorporeal deliverances transcending all corporeality; nor, after wisely understanding things, have his taints been destroyed. But he has a certain degree of faith in the Perfect One, a certain degree of devotion to him, and he possesses such faculties as faith, energy, mindfulness, concentration, and wisdom. Such a one, O monks, is called a faith-devotee.

AN 3:21

One cannot, Sāriputta, definitely say that one of these three beings (the body-witness, the one attained to understanding, and the one liberated by faith) is the higher and superior one.

For it may well be that one who is liberated by faith is on the path to arahatship while the body-witness and one who has attained to understanding are once-returners or never-returners.

Or it may be that one who is a body-witness is on the path to arahatship, while the one liberated by faith and one attained to understanding are once-returners or never-returners.

Or it may be that one who has attained to understanding is on the path to arahatship, while the one liberated by faith and the body-witness are once-returners or never-returners.

§ 201 Four Ways of Progress

According to the way in which the equanimity knowledge is attained—with toil or with ease, slowly or quickly—four ways of progress are distinguished.

AN 4:162

There are, O monks, four ways of progress (*paṭipadā*), namely:

1. toilsome progress accompanied by slow comprehension (*dukkhapaṭipadā dandhābhiññā*);
2. toilsome progress accompanied by quick comprehension (*dukkhapaṭipadā khippābhiññā*);
3. easy progress accompanied by slow comprehension (*sukhapaṭipadā dandhābhiññā*);

4. easy progress accompanied by quick comprehension (*sukhapaṭipadā khippābhiññā*).

1. But what, O monks, is toilsome progress accompanied by slow comprehension? Here, O monks, someone possesses by nature intense greed, intense hate, and intense delusion; and thereby he frequently experiences suffering and grief. Also the five mental faculties (faith, energy, mindfulness, concentration, wisdom) are weakly developed in him; and therefore he reaches only slowly the immediate condition to the destruction of the taints.

2. But what, O monks, is toilsome progress accompanied by quick comprehension? Here, O monks, someone possesses by nature intense greed, intense hate, and intense delusion; and thereby he frequently experiences suffering and grief. But the five mental faculties are strongly developed in him; and therefore he quickly reaches the immediate condition to the destruction of the taints.

3. But what, O monks, is easy progress accompanied by slow comprehension? Here, O monks, someone does not possess by nature intense greed, hate, or delusion; and thereby he only rarely experiences suffering and grief. The five mental faculties, however, are only weakly developed in him; and therefore he reaches only slowly the immediate condition to the destruction of the taints.

4. But what, O monks, is easy progress accompanied by quick comprehension? Here, O monks, someone does not possess by nature intense greed, hate, or delusion; and thereby he only rarely experiences suffering and grief. Also the five mental faculties are strongly developed in him; and therefore he quickly reaches the immediate condition to the destruction of the taints.

By the "immediate condition" (*ānantariya*) is meant the mental concentration associated with the path of arahatship immediately followed by the fruit of arahatship. Of this state it is said in Snp 226:

There is no concentration that would ever equal
The stainless concentration that the Buddha praised,

Which the "immediate gate" to holiness is called:
By this Dhamma may there be safety.

The above mentioned five mental faculties are the necessary equipment for the successful development of insight (*vipassanā*), on which depends the way of progress.

AN 4:163 gives the same explanations, but with regard to the second way of progress it further says that the monk toils by contemplating the loathsomeness of body and food, the undesirability of all existence, impermanence, and death; while, regarding the third and fourth ways of progress, the monk enjoys the *jhānas*.

According to AN 4:167–68 Moggallāna reached arahatship through the second way of progress, Sāriputta through the fourth.

§202 **(9) Adaptation knowledge**

One who possesses equanimity regarding all formations is unshakable in faith, energy, mindfulness, concentration, and wisdom. As this ninth knowledge reviews the results of the eight preceding knowledges, and adapts itself to the things belonging to the path and enlightenment, therefore it is called adaptation knowledge, the transitional stage to the entry upon the four supramundane paths (see Vism XXI,128–33).

THE THIRTY-SEVEN STATES LEADING TO ENLIGHTENMENT

(bodhipakkiyā dhammā)
MN 77

(1–4) And further, Udāyi, I have shown to my disciples the way to develop the four applications of mindfulness (*satipaṭṭhāna*):

Here the monk dwells in contemplation of the body ... feeling ... mind ... mind-objects, ardent, clearly conscious and mindful, after putting away worldly greed and grief.

(5–8) And further I have shown them the way to develop the four right efforts (*sammāppadhāna*): Here the monk incites his will, strives, puts forth his energy, strains his mind in order to avoid the arising of evil, unwholesome states ... to overcome them ... to arouse wholesome states ... to bring them to growth and full development.

(9–12) And further I have shown them the way to develop the four roads to power (*iddhipāda*): Here the monk develops the road to power accompanied by concentration of will ... energy ... mind ... reflection.

(13–17) And further I have shown them the way to develop the five mental faculties (*indriya*): Here the monk develops faith ... energy ... mindfulness ... concentration ... wisdom, leading to peace and enlightenment.

(18–22) And further I have shown them the way to develop the five mental powers (*bala*): Here the monk develops the power of faith ... energy ... mindfulness ... concentration ... wisdom, leading to peace and enlightenment.

(23–29) And further I have shown them the way to develop the seven factors of enlightenment (*bojjhaṅga*): Here the monk develops the factors of enlightenment bent on solitude, on detachment, on cessation, and ending in deliverance, namely: mindfulness ... investigation of phenomena ... energy ... rapture ... tranquillity ... concentration ... equanimity.

(30–37) And further I have shown them the way to develop the Noble Eightfold Path (*ariya-aṭṭhaṅgika-magga*): Here the monk develops right understanding, right thought, right speech, right action, right livelihood, right effort, right mindfulness, and right concentration.

§203 **VII. Purity of knowledge and vision**
(*ñāṇadassana-visuddhi*)

By this stage of purity is meant the penetrating and experiential knowledge of the four supramundane paths (*magga-ñāṇa*), namely: the path of stream-entry (*sotāpatti-magga*), the path of once-return (*sakadāgāmi-magga*), the path of never-return (*anāgāmi-magga*), and the path of arahatship (*arahatta-magga*).

As soon as every form of existence has appeared to the mind as an obstacle, then, immediately after the adaptation knowledge (*anuloma-ñāṇa*), there arises the maturity knowledge (*gotrabhū-ñāṇa*). And while taking as object the signless, the standstill, the non-becoming, the cessation, Nibbāna, this knowledge transcends the rank (*gotta* = *gotra*), name, and sphere of the worldling (*puthujjana*) and enters into the rank, name, and sphere of the noble ones (*ariya*), and thereby forms the first turning towards Nibbāna as object, the first thinking about it, the first concentration on it. This, therefore, is the maturity knowledge, which forms the summit of insight and never arises a second time (see Vism XXII,5).

Pṭs I.66

But for what reason is the knowledge of turning away and detachment from all external things considered as "maturity knowledge" (*gotrabhū-ñāṇa*)? Because it overcomes the arising of existence, the progress of existence ... of despair ... the condition consisting in external formations, and because it drives towards no-more-arising, to the standstill of the process of existence ... to the end of despair, to cessation, to Nibbāna; because it overcomes the arising of existence and drives towards no-more-arising.

Immediately following maturity knowledge, there arises that state of consciousness called the "path" (*magga-citta*: path-consciousness), bursting asunder and destroying the mass of greed, hate, and ignorance which never had been burst and destroyed before (cf. Vism XXII, 11–14).

§204 The Ten Fetters and the Four Paths

SN 45:179–80

There are, O monks, five lower fetters (*saṃyojana*), namely: (1) personality view, (2) sceptical doubt, (3) attachment to rules and rituals, (4) sensual greed, (5) anger (*sakkāya-diṭṭhi*, *vicikicchā, silabbata-parāmāsa, kāma-rāga, paṭigha).*

And there are five higher fetters, namely: (6) greed for fine-material existence, (7) greed for immaterial existence, (8) conceit, (9) restlessness, (10) ignorance (*rūpa-rāga, arūpa-raga, māna, uddhacca, avijjā*).

AN 4:239

1. Here, O monks, with the vanishing of the three fetters (1–3), the monk is a stream-enterer (*sotāpanna*), who has forever escaped the states of woe, is affirmed, assured of final enlightenment.

2. With the vanishing of the three fetters and the attenuation of greed, hate, and delusion, the monk is a once-returner (*sakadāgāmi*). And returning to this world only once more, he puts an end to suffering.

3. With the vanishing of the five lower fetters, the monk is due to be reborn in a higher world, and there he reaches Nibbāna, no more returning (*anāgāmi*) from that world.

4. But with the vanishing of all taints (and the ten fetters) he reaches already in this world the liberation of mind and the liberation through wisdom, after realizing and understanding it in his own person.

> Immediately following the path-consciousness of any of the four stages of sanctity, there springs up, as its result, the so-called fruition-consciousness (*phala-citta*) which may also later on be repeated after practising insight (*vipassanā*). The path-consciousness of each of the four stages of sanctity, however, arises only once, forming, as it were, the entrance to one of the four stages of sanctity.
>
> In the moments of "reviewing" (*paccavekkhaṇa*) following upon the fruition moments, the monk understands the fetters which have been overcome, and those which still have to be overcome.

§205 The Simultaneous Understanding of the Truths

Pṭs. I,119

The understanding of one endowed with the path is, at the same time, also the understanding of the truth of suffering, of the origin of suffering, of the cessation of suffering, and of the path leading to the cessation of suffering.

The Early Masters (cited at Vism XXII,92)

Just as a light, at one and the same moment, performs simultaneously four functions: burning the wick, dispelling darkness, producing light, and consuming oil; just so the path-knowledge (*magga-ñāṇa*) masters in one and the same moment simultaneously all Four Noble Truths.

It masters suffering by fully comprehending it (*pariññā*); masters the origin of suffering by overcoming it (*pahāna*); masters the Eightfold Path by developing it (*bhāvanā*); masters the cessation of suffering by realizing it (*sacchikiriya*). And what does this mean? It means that the knowledge which has cessation as its object comprehends, beholds and penetrates, at the same time, all the Four Noble Truths.

AN 3:25

Just, O monks, as a man with good eyes, in the gloom and darkness of the night, at the sudden flashing up of lightning, might recognize the objects; just so the monk sees according to reality: "This is suffering, this is the origin of suffering, this is the cessation of suffering, this is the path leading to the cessation of suffering."

SUPPLEMENT

§206 Cessation of Consciousness

(*nirodha-samāpatti*)

Here a certain meditative attainment will be dealt with which is often referred to in the Suttas. It is the so-called "attainment of cessation" (*nirodha-samāpatti*), or "cessation of perception and feeling" (*saññā-vedayita-nirodha*), i.e. the temporary suspension of all mental activity, which may last seven days and even longer. According to the Comy. it may be attained only by a never-returner or arahat who has mastered all the eight *jhānas* (see B. Dict.). This attainment, however, is not essential for the realization of arahatship.

SN 36:11

For one who has entered the first *jhāna*, speech has ceased. For one who has entered the second *jhāna*, thought conception and discursive thinking have ceased. For one who has entered the third *jhāna*, rapture has ceased. For one who has entered the fourth *jhāna*, in-and-out breathing has ceased. For one who has entered the sphere of boundless space, the perception of forms has ceased. For one who has entered the sphere of boundless consciousness, the perception of the sphere of boundless space has ceased. For one who has entered the sphere of nothingness, the perception of the sphere of boundless consciousness has ceased. For one who has entered the sphere of neither-perception-nor-non-perception, the perception of the sphere of nothingness has ceased. For one who has entered the cessation of perception and feeling, perception and feeling have ceased.

MN 44

"Now, in which way, Venerable One (Visākha asks his former wife Dhammadinnā), does the entrance into the cessation of perception and feeling take place?"

"Here, Brother Visākha, the monk in entering into the cessation of perception and feeling does not think: 'I shall enter into the cessation of perception and feeling'; or: 'I am entering into it'; or: 'I have entered into it.' But already previously, his mind has been developed in such a way that it simply inclines toward such a state."

"Now, which things, Venerable One, are first extinguished in the monk entering into the cessation of perception and feeling: the bodily function (*kāyasaṅkhāra* = in-and-out-breathing), or the verbal function (*vacī-saṅkhāra* = thought conception and discursive thinking), or the mind function (*citta-saṅkhāra* = perception and feeling)?"

"The verbal function becomes first extinguished (in the first *jhāna*), then the bodily function (in the fourth *jhāna*), then the mind function (on entering cessation)."

"In which way, Venerable One, does the rising from the cessation of perception and feeling take place?"

"Here, Brother Visākha, the monk on rising from the cessation of perception and feeling does not think: 'I shall rise from the cessation of perception and feeling'; or: 'I am rising from it'; or: 'I have arisen from it'. But already previously to that, his mind has been developed in such a way that it simply inclines toward such a state."

"But, Venerable One, what arises first in the monk rising from the cessation of perception and feeling: the bodily function, or the verbal function, or the mind function?"

"First arises the mind function (in the eighth *jhāna*), then the bodily function (in the third jhana), then the verbal function (in the first jhana)."

"How many impressions, Venerable One, come to the monk after rising from the cessation of perception and feeling?"

"Three impressions, Brother Visākha: the impression of emptiness, of signlessness, of desirelessness."

"But towards what, Venerable One, inclines the mind of such a monk? At what does it aim? To what is it directed?"

"His mind inclines towards detachment, aims at detachment, is directed to detachment."

MN 43

"What, O brother, is the difference between a dead man and a monk who has entered into the cessation of perception and feeling?"

"In the dead man the bodily, verbal, and mental functions are extinguished and have come to rest, life is exhausted, the warmth has disappeared, the sense organs are destroyed. In the monk, however, who has entered into the cessation of perception and feeling, the bodily, verbal, and mental functions have become extinguished and come to rest, but life is not exhausted, warmth has not disappeared, and the sense organs are stilled. This is the difference between a dead man and a monk who has entered into the cessation of perception and feeling."

INDEX

A

Abhibhāyatana, eight 69, 121:-*See also Mastery, eight stages of*
Abhiññā 106, 124, 125:-*See also Spiritual powers*
Abodes, four divine (brahma-vihāra) 65, 93, 102, 105
Actions and their results (kamma) 11, 17, 20, 21, 22, 36, 148, 151, 153
Ādīnavānupassanā 169:-*See also Misery, contemplation of*
Adaptation-knowledge (anuloma-ñāṇa) 169, 178, 180
Advertence (āvajjana & manasikāra) 72, 132, 137, 150
Āhāra-paṭikūla-saññā 111:-*See also Food, loathsomeness of*
Ājīva-pārisuddhi-sīla 57:-*See also Livelihood, purity of*
Ākāsānañcāyatana 107:-*See also Boundless space*
Ākiñcaññāyatana 109:-*See also Nothingness, sphere of*
Akusala 53, 133, 137, 143:-*See also [karmically] Unwholesome*
Āloka-saññā 70:-*See also Light, perception of*
Anāgāmi 180, 181:-*See also Never-return, path of*
Ānantarika kamma 37:-*See also Immediate results*
Ānantariya 177:-*See also Immediate condition*
Ānāpānasati 83:-*See also Breathing, mindfulness of*
Anattā 64, 87, 129, 161, 166:-*See also Impersonality, Non-self, & Selflessness*
° -lakkhaṇa 14
Anicca 64, 87, 129, 160, 166:-*See also Impermanence*
Aññā 138, 143:-*See also Gnosis*
Annihilation view (uccheda-vāda or vibhava-diṭṭhi) 7, 146
Anubodha 144:-*See also Comprehension*
Anuloma-ñāṇa 169, 180:-*See also Adaptation-knowledge*
Anussati, ten 65, 71:-*See also Contemplation*
Appamaññā 93:-*See also Boundless states, four*
Arūpāyatana, four 65, 107:-*See also Immaterial spheres*
Arising and passing (udayabbayā) 41, 169
Ariya-puggala 27, 41, 64, 129, 143:-*See also Holiness, four stages of*
Ariya-saccā, four 5:-*See also Noble truths, four*
Āsava 151, 174:-*See also Taints*
° -(k)khaya 125
Ascetic practices (dhutaṅga) 58-60
Attachment-Groups (upādāna-kkhandha) 6, 121, 146, 159, 160, 169
Āvajjana 137:-*See also Advertence*
Avijjā 15, 23, 151, 152, 160, 163, 18 1:-*See also Ignorance*
Avyākata 133, 137, 143:-*See also [karmically] Neutral*
Āyatana, six or twelve 15, 130, 135:-*See also Sense bases*

B

Bala 106, 159, 179:-*See also Mindfulness, as one of the mental powers*

Bhaṅgānupassanā 169:–*See also Dissolution, contemplation on*
Bhavaṅga 136, 138:–*See also Subconsciousness*
Bhāvanā 41, 63-64, 101-102, 182:–*See also Development*
° -mayā-paññā 129
asubha- ° 70
karuṇā- ° 101
mettā- ° 93
muditā- ° 101
paññā- ° 64, 129
samādhi- ° 64
samatha- ° 64
upekkhā- ° 102
vipassanā- ° 64
Bhayatupaṭṭhāna 169:–*See also Terror, awareness of*
Bodhipakkiyā dhammā 178:–*See also Enlightenment, states leading to*
Body, contemplation on (kāyānupassanā) 9, 65, 69-73, 76-77, 80-83, 84, 89, 90, 114-118, 119, 122-124, 131, 136, 138, 139, 142, 155, 157, 159, 162, 163, 171, 178
Body-witness (kāya-sakkhī) 174, 175, 176-177
Bojjhaṅga, seven 90-91, 159, 179:–*See also Enlightenment, seven factors of*
Both-ways liberated (ubhatobhāga-vimutta) 174
Boundless consciousness, sphere of (viññāṇañcāyatana) 27, 65, 92, 104-105, 109, 110, 120, 183
Boundless space, sphere of (ākāsānañcāyatana) 27, 65, 92, 104, 107, 109, 110, 120, 183
Boundless states, four (brahma-vihāra) 93-103, 105
Brahma-vihāra 65, 93:–*See also Abodes, four divine*
Breathing, mindfulness of (ānāpāna-sati) 65, 71, 76, 83, 85, 86, 88-89, 115, 116, 121, 123, 124, 183, 184
Buddha, contemplation on 65, 72-73, 73

C

Cemetery meditation 70, 72
Cessation (nirodha) 14, 23, 33, 34, 40, 71-72, 91, 110, 112, 139, 156, 158, 166, 179, 180, 182
as Nibbāna-aspect 26-27
contemplation of ° 85, 87, 89, 91, 123
in Dependent Origination 23-24, 154
of becoming (bhava-nirodha) 92, 93
of consciousness (nirodha-samāpatti) 175, 183
of defilements (kilesa-parinibbāna) 91
of greed, hate, & delusion (lobha, dosa, & moha) 24
of groups of existence (khandha-parinibbāna) 33, 88, 91
of ignorance (avijjā) 151-154, 164
of karma (kamma) 22, 154, 162, 163, 164
of perception & feeling (saññā-vedayita-nirodha) 121, 183-185
of suffering (dukkha) 5-8, 10, 32, 33, 40, 43, 73, 119, 142, 144-150, 154, 155, 162, 182
of taints (āsavakkhaya) 125-126, 152
Cetanā 53, 132, 150, 151, 153, 164:–*See also Volition*
Cetasika 132, 150:–*See also Consciousness*
Characteristics of existence, three (lakkhaṇa) 13, 156
Citta 133, 136, 150, 151, 180, 181:–*See also Conciousness & Mind*
Citta-saṅkhāra 87, 89, 184:–*See*

also Mental formation
Citt'ekaggatā 41, 63, 147:–*See also One-pointedness of mind*
Clinging (upādāna) 7, 15, 23, 27, 45-47, 92, 112, 122, 123, 146, 147, 150, 151, 154, 159, 160, 162, 165, 169
Community of Noble Disciples (Saṅgha) 142
  contemplation on ° 65
Compassion (karuṇā) 65, 93, 97, 102, 103, 106, 106-107, 121, 133
  development of ° 101-102, 104
Comprehension (anubodha) 34, 144
  clear ° 77, 89
  full ° (pariññā) 182
  mundane ° 144, 145
  quick ° 176, 177
  slow ° 176, 177
Concentration (samādhi) 24, 41, 42, 56, 63, 64, 66, 67, 70, 72, 74, 81, 83, 83-86, 92, 115, 129, 132, 151, 173, 177, 179, 180
  in widest sense 41, 63, 143
  as part of threefold division of the Path 41, 42, 43, 44
  as part of noble eightfold path: right-concentration 5, 8, 9, 10, 33, 41, 63, 72, 147, 152, 159, 163, 164, 179
  as part of the spiritual faculties (indriya & bala) 138, 141-143, 175, 176, 177, 178, 179
  as factor of enlightenment (samādhi-sambojjhaṅga) 40, 90, 112, 119, 179
  exercises (kammaṭṭhāna) 64
  preliminary ° 63, 66
  neighbourhood ° 63, 65, 67, 76, 109, 110
  absorption ° or attainment ° 63, 67, 83-84, 102, 107, 109
Consciousness 23, 24, 33, 63, 70, 81, 109, 111-112, 130, 132, 133, 135, 136, 144, 150-151, 153, 154, 157, 158, 159, 165, 167, 169, 181:–*See also Viññāṇa, Citta, & Cetasika*
  ° -kasiṇa 65, 68
  cessation of 175, 183
  clear ° (sampajañña) 116, 117, 118, 119, 120
  in Dependent Origination 134-135, 146, 150, 152, 154, 166
  in relation to the three characteristics of existence 14, 15, 87, 166
  its sensory conditions 79, 80, 121, 136, 137
  karmically wholesome °/unwholesome ° 10, 63, 133, 137, 143, 163
  path ° (magga-citta) 180, 181
Consciousness group (viññāṇa-kkhandha) 5, 7, 13-14, 31, 32, 33, 41, 64, 72, 99, 119, 121, 129, 130, 131, 133-135, 146, 157, 160, 172, 173
Contemplation (anussati) 9, 65, 75, 81, 89, 100-102, 109, 110, 111, 173
  cemetery ° 65, 72
  on body, feelings, mind, mind objects 89, 90, 115-120:–*See also Satipaṭṭhāna*
  ten (anussati) 65, 71-72
    ° of the Buddha 73
    ° of the doctrine 73
    ° of the community 74
    ° of morality 74
    ° of liberality 74
    ° of heavenly beings 74-75
    ° of death 75-82
    ° of the body 81-83
    ° of breathing 83-91
    ° of peace 91-93
  ten (saññā) 121-124:–*See also Girimānanda Sutta*
Conventional language (vohāra-vacana) 33, 162:–*See also Ultimate truth*
Corporeality group (rūpakkhandha) 7, 73, 88, 99, 130, 131, 134, 146, 160
Craving (taṇhā) 6-8, 11-13, 16-17, 22

-23, 23, 27, 28, 30, 73, 87, 91, 92, 123, 146, 159, 160, 165
in Dependent Origination 15, 23, 147, 150, 154
Crimes, five hellish 37

D

Dāna 105:-*See also Liberality*
Death (maraṇā) 11, 20, 23, 27-28, 37, 91, 94, 152, 154, 156, 165, 169
as heavenly messenger (deva-dūta) 10
contemplation on (maraṇānu-sati) 65, 71, 75-82, 178
does the Buddha continue after ° 32, 33
Māra as ° 34
Defilement of insight (vipassan'ūpa-kkilesa) 167
Deliverance (nibbāna, vimokkha, & vimutti) 6, 24, 27, 40, 42, 43, 56, 86, 88, 91, 104, 105, 107, 125, 160, 163, 172, 179
desire for ° (muccitukamyatā) 169, 172, 174
eightfold ° (aṭṭha vimokkha) 120-121
threefold ° 173, 174
three gates to ° 173
Delusion (moha) 6, 21-22, 24, 26, 27, 29, 34, 35, 75, 92, 124, 133, 155, 177-178, 181
Dependent origination (paṭic-ca-samuppāda) 6, 14, 16, 23, 130, 134, 146, 150-156, 160, 164, 166
Desireless deliverance (appaṇihita-vimokkha) 173, 174
Detachment (virāga) 7, 9, 23, 25, 34, 40, 56, 59, 71-72, 80, 91, 92, 112, 142, 146, 157, 179, 180, 185
contemplation of ° 85, 85-89, 121, 123
Development (bhāvanā) 10, 41, 44, 63-64, 67, 72, 73, 93, 101-102, 103-105, 125, 129-130, 178
Dhammānusārī 174:-*See also Truth devotee*
Dhamma 31, 42, 75, 90, 142, 178:-*See also Doctrine*
contemplation of ° 71, 73
equation with Dependent origination (paṭicca-samup-pāda) 134, 146
investigation of ° (dham-ma-vicaya-sambojjhaṅga) 40, 90, 112, 119, 179
Dhamma-vicaya 40, 90:-*See also Dhamma, investigation of*
Dhātu 109, 130, 136, 137:-*See also Elements*
° -vavatthāna 114, 117, 131
Dhutaṅga 58-60:-*See also Ascetic practices*
Dibba-cakkhu 70, 125:-*See also Divine eye*
Disciples, the seven noble 174
Discursive thinking (vicāra) 9, 67, 68, 87, 102, 132, 137, 183, 184
Dissolution, contemplation on (bhaṅgānupassanā) 86, 169
Divine eye (dibba-cakkhu) 70, 125
Diṭṭhi
° -patta (attained to under-standing) 174
° -sampayutta (wrong view) 164
° -visuddhi 44, 155, 168:-*See also Purity, of understanding*
sakkāya- ° (personality view) 162, 180
sammā- ° 5, 8, 145:-*See also Right understanding*
sassata- ° 7, 146:-*See also Eternity view*
uccheda- ° 146:-*See also Annihilation view*
vibhava- ° 7:-*See also Annihilation view*
Doctrine (Dhamma)
contemplation of ° 65, 73

Domanassa 138, 140:–*See also Sadness, Pain, & Grief*
Dosa 21, 26, 70:–*See also Hate*
Dukkha 64, 87, 129, 138, 160, 166:–*See also Suffering, Pain & Unsatisfactoriness*
Dull natured (moha-carita) 70

E

Effort, right (vāyāma, sammā) 5, 8-9, 33, 43, 147-148, 152, 159, 163, 164, 179
  the four (sammāppadhāna) 40-41, 179
Elements (dhātu) 76, 155, 165
  the eighteen 130, 137-138
  the four primary 65, 73, 83, 114, 117, 131, 150
Emptiness (suññatā) 110, 184
  fourfold 172
Energy (viriya) 9, 40, 58, 77, 89-91, 97, 105, 112, 119, 132, 138, 141-142, 142, 167, 175, 176, 177, 178, 179
Enlightenment (bodhi) 33, 40, 71, 91, 141, 178, 181
  seven factors of ° (bojjhaṅga) 9, 40, 88, 89-90, 103-105, 112, 119, 159
  states leading to ° (bodhipakkiyā dhammā) 179
Equanimity (upekkhā) 9, 10, 40, 77-78, 89, 97, 106, 107, 111, 140-141, 174, 176
  ° regarding all formations (saṅkhār'upekkhā) 169, 173, 178
  as a defilement of insight 167
  as a divine abode or boundless state 93
  as a factor of enlightnement 65, 90, 112, 119, 179
  as a jhāna factor 68, 87, 107
  development of ° 102-106
Escape from doubt, purity of (kaṅkhāvitaraṇa-visuddhi) 45-47, 160, 161, 162, 168
Eternity view (sassata-diṭṭhi) 7, 146
Extremes, the two 33, 146:–*See also Path, middle*
  self-mortification 14, 33, 39
  sensual pleasure 33, 39

F

Faculties (indriya)
  the five mental/spiritual ° 141-143, 159, 175, 176, 177-178, 179
  the twenty-two ° 130, 138-145
Faith (saddhā) 58, 74, 133, 138, 141, 142, 174, 175, 176, 177, 178, 179
  ° devotee (saddhānusāri) 174, 176
  liberated by ° (saddhā-vimutta) 174, 175
Feeling (vedanā) 9, 28, 68, 80-81, 87, 100, 134, 135, 145, 150, 153, 157, 165, 166, 169
  as a link in Dependent Origination 15, 23, 146-147, 150, 154
  as one of five groups of existence (vedanākkhandha) 5, 7, 13-14, 31-33, 41, 64, 72, 88, 99, 110, 111, 119, 121, 129, 130, 132, 134, 140, 160:–*See also Attachment-Groups*
  as one of the four satipaṭṭhānas 88
  cessation of ° 183-185
  contemplation of ° 89, 90, 118, 172, 173, 178
  threefold division of ° 132, 140, 157, 159
  fivefold division of ° 140, 146
Fetters, ten (saṃyojana) 26, 27, 162, 180-181
Food (āhāra) 39, 58, 76, 77
  as alms 18, 19, 20, 106
  loathsomeness of ° 65, 111-112, 113-114, 178

proper use of ° 55, 57, 112-113
Fruition-consciousness (phala-citta) 181

G

Girimānanda Sutta 121-124
Gladness (somanassa) 38, 138-140
Gnosis (aññā) 138, 139, 143
Gotrabhū-ñāṇa 180:–*See also Maturity knowledge*
Greed (lobha) 9, 21-22, 24, 26, 27, 29, 34, 35-36, 40, 58, 59, 75, 92, 97, 99, 100, 103, 106, 113, 118, 124, 133, 159, 177-178, 180, 181
worldly ° and grief (abhijjhādomanassa) 9, 89-90, 116, 142, 178
Grief (domanassa) 6, 7, 9, 16, 23, 24, 40, 52, 75, 89-90, 116, 120, 142, 147, 150, 155, 177-178, 178
Groups of existence, five (pañca khandha) 5, 6, 26-28, 33, 73, 88, 130, 134, 146, 150, 155, 170
cessation of ° (khandha-parinibbāna) 27, 91

H

Hate (dosa) 21-22, 24, 26, 29, 34, 35-36, 92, 93-101, 107, 133, 177-178, 180, 181
Hearsay, do not go by mere 35:–*See also Kālāma Sutta*
Heavenly beings 94, 156, 164
contemplation on 65, 71, 74-75
Hindrances, five (nīvaraṇa) 67-68, 72, 87, 109-110, 119, 125
Holiness, four stages of (ariya-puggala) 64, 178
Hymn of Love (Metta Sutta) 99-100

I

Iddhipāda 159, 179:–*See also Power, four roads to*
Ignorance (avijjā) 11-13, 15-16, 22-23, 29, 64, 129, 146, 147, 150, 151-153, 154, 163, 164, 165, 180
Images, mental (nimitta) 41, 69, 71, 86, 107-108
acquired ° (uggaha-nimitta) 66, 67, 69, 83
counter- ° (paṭibhāga-nimitta) 66, 67, 83, 86
Immaterial spheres (arūpāyatana, four) 65, 107, 111
Immediate condition (ānantariya) 177
Immediate results (ānantarika kamma) 37
Impermanence (anicca) 25, 64, 69, 88, 89, 124, 129, 132, 145, 167, 178
contemplation on ° 85, 87-88, 121-122, 123, 173
Impersonality (anattā) 5, 34
Indifference (upekkhā) 76, 90, 138, 140
faculty of ° (upekkh'indriya) 140
Indriya 130, 138, 159, 179:–*See also Faculties*
Indriya-saṃvara-sīla 57
Insight (vipassanā) 43, 64-65, 95, 97, 115, 166, 180, 181
development of ° 125, 129-130, 160, 178
exercises for both tranquility and insight 81-88, 159
nine kinds of ° knowledge 168-179
six objects of ° 130, 155
starting point for ° 72-73
ten defilements of ° (vipassan'ūpakkilesa) 167
Intoxicants 51, 52

J

Jhāna 64, 66, 67, 68, 72, 95, 102, 125, 130, 137, 175, 178, 183-185:–*See also Concentration, absorption or attainment & Samādhi, appanā-*

four material absorptions
9, 10, 43, 65, 142, 183
four immaterial spheres
107-108
methods of attaining °
awareness of breathing
83, 86-87
contemplation of body, 32
parts of 83-84
development of equanimity 102
kasiṇa 66-68, 69
Joy, altruistic (muditā)
65, 93, 102, 103, 124, 133
development of °
101, 104-105, 106-107

K

Kālāma Sutta 35-37
Kamma, (Skt. karma)
17, 21, 22, 36, 37, 39, 151:–*See also Actions and their results*
° -bhava 154
Kammaṭṭhāna 64:–*See also Concentration, exercises*
Kaṅkhāvītaraṇa-visuddhi 44, 160:–*See also Escape from doubt*
Kappa (Skt. kalpa) 12, 167:–*See also World-period*
Karma-formations (saṅkhārā) 15, 23, 91, 123, 146-147, 153, 163, 165
as conditions of existence
170, 171
in Dependent origination
150, 154
three types 151-152
Karma (volitional activities) 6, 97, 122, 133, 151, 153, 164, 165, 173:–*See also Actions and their results*
° -born (kammaja) 163
° -result 133, 150, 153, 154, 162, 164, 165
° process (kamma-bhava)
15, 16, 23, 147, 150, 154, 165
° & rebirth (uppatti-bhava)
6, 17, 154, 160, 162, 163, 165
round of ° 165
Karuṇā 65, 101:–*See also Compassion*
Kasiṇa exercises 65-71, 107, 108:–*See also Concentration & Jhana, methods of attaining*
Kāyānupassanā 81:–*See also Body, contemplation on*
Kāya
° -gatāsati 81:–*See also Body, contemplation on*
° -saṅkhāra 184
° -sakkhī 174:–*See also Body-witness*
° -sañcetanā 163:–*See also Volition, manifested in body*
° -viññatti 132
Khandha-parinibbāna 27, 91:–*See also Groups of existence, cessation ofSee also Nibbāna, saupādisesa- ° & anupādisesa- °*
Kilesa-parinibbāna 27, 91:–*See also Nibbāna, saupādisesa- ° & anupādisesa- °*
Kindness, all embracing (mettā)
65, 97, 100, 101, 102, 103, 124:–*See also Abodes, four divine*
as one of the ten perfections
(pāramī) 106-108
development of °
93-95, 103-104
Kinship with all 13
Kusala 53, 133, 137:–*See also [karmically] Wholesome*

L

Liberality (dāna)
65, 71, 74, 75, 105-106
Light, perception of (āloka-saññā)
70
Livelihood (ājīva)
right ° (sammā-ājīva)
5, 8, 147-148
as part of noble eightfold path

8, 33, 43-44, 152, 163, 164, 179
purity of ° (ājīva-pārisuddhi-sīla) 57, 159
impurity of ° 57, 58, 133
Lobha 21:–*See also Greed*
Lokiya 125, 130, 147:–*See also Mundane*
Lokuttara 125, 130, 147, 148:–*See also Supramundane*
Lust (rāga) 7, 72, 122, 159
sensual ° (kāmacchanda) 40, 67, 87, 119, 125
Lustful nature (rāga-carita) 70

M

Māra 34, 169
Magga 41, 149:–*See also Path*
ariya-aṭṭhaṅgika- ° 179:–*See also Path, noble eightfold*
sotāpatti- ° 179:–*See also Path, of stream-entry*
sakadāgāmi- ° 179:–*See also Path, of once-return*
anāgāmi- ° 180:–*See also Path, of never-return*
arahatta- ° 180:–*See also Path, of arahatship*
° -citta 180:–*See also Conciousness, path*
° -ñāṇa 179, 182:–*See also Path-knowledge*
Manasikāra 132, 150:–*See also Advertence*
Manāyatana 136:–*See also Mind-base*
Mano:–*See Mind*
° -dhātu 109, 136
° -dvāra 136
° -sañcetanā 163:–*See also Volition, manifested in mind*
° -viññāṇa 109, 136
bhavaṅga- ° 138:–*See also Subconsciousness*
Maraṇānusati 75:–*See also Death, contemplation on*
Mastery, eight stages of (abhibhāyatana) 69-70
Maturity knowledge (gotrabhū-ñāṇa) 180
Meat-eating 53
Mentally unsteady nature (vitakka-carita) 70
Mental formation (citta-saṅkhāra) 87-89, 135, 166
as factor of ānāpānasati 84, 85
as one of five groups of existence 5, 7, 13, 14, 31-33, 41, 64, 72, 99, 119, 121, 129, 130-132, 134, 140, 146, 157, 160, 166, 169, 172, 173
cessation of ° 14
Mental pain (domanassa) 24, 52
Messengers, three heavenly (devadūta) 10
Mettā 65, 93, 106:–*See also Kindness, all embracing*
Mind-base (manāyatana) 135-136, 150
Mindfulness (sati) 10, 76, 77, 133, 142, 178
° of in-and-out breathing (ānāpānasati) 84-86, 88-89, 121, 123, 124
as factor of enlightenment (sati-sambojjhaṅga) 40, 90-91, 112, 179
as one of the mental faculties (indriya) & mental powers (bala) 138, 141, 175, 176, 177, 179
as part of noble eightfold path: right-mindfulness 5, 8, 9, 33, 43, 147-148, 152, 159, 163, 164, 179
the four applications of ° (satipaṭṭhāna) 41, 88, 89, 115-120, 142, 178
Mind (citta & mano) 6, 24, 37, 39, 41, 51, 63, 64, 73, 85, 107, 131

° -consciousness (manoviññāṇa) 80, 109, 133, 136, 137, 138, 157, 159
° -element (mano-dhātu) 109, 136-137
° -function (citta-saṅkhāra) 184
as sixth sense base (manāyatana) 13, 135, 138, 139
contemplation of ° (cittānupassana) 9, 88, 118
door of ° (manodvāra) 136
Mind and corporeality (nāma-rūpa) 15, 23, 146, 147, 150, 150-151, 153, 154, 165
Misery, contemplation of (ādīnavānupassanā) 121, 122-123, 159, 169, 170-171
Moha 21:–*See also Delusion*
° -carita 70:–*See also Dull natured*
Monk's Discipline 8, 42, 43, 57-61:–*See also Pātimokkha*
Morality (sīla) 51, 52, 55-57, 74, 143, 155
as one of the ten perfections (pāramī) 105
as part of threefold division of the Path 41, 42, 43, 44, 63
contemplation of ° 65, 71
training in higher ° (adhisīla-sikkhā) 42, 43, 44-47, 86
Muccitukamyatā 169:–*See also Deliverance, desire for*
Muditā 65, 101:–*See also Joy, altruistic*
Mundane (lokiya) 72, 125, 130, 145, 147, 148

N

Ñāṇadassana-visuddhi 179:–*See also Purity, of knowledge and vision*
Nāma-rūpa 15, 23, 150, 152, 153, 155, 165, 168:–*See also Mind and corporeality*
Nature, inflexible law of 11
Neither-perception-nor-non-perception, sphere of (neva-saññā-n' āsaññāyatana) 27, 65, 110, 120, 121, 183
[karmically] Neutral (avyākata) 133, 137, 143
Neva-saññā-n' āsaññāyatana 110:–*See also Neither-perception-nor-non-perception, sphere of*
Never-return, path of (anāgāmi) 107, 112
Nibbāna 6, 23-30, 33, 40, 45-47, 71, 88, 97, 116, 120, 123, 145, 151, 158, 171, 173, 180, 181:–*See also Deliverance*
contemplation of ° 91-93
saupādisesa- ° & anupādisesa- ° 26-27
Nimitta 69, 160, 170:–*See also Images, mental*
paṭibhāga- ° 66, 67, 83
uggaha- ° 66, 67, 83
Nirodha 88:–*See also Cessation*
° -samāpatti 183:–*See also Cessation, of consciousness*
bhava- ° 92:–*See also Cessation, of becoming*
saññā-vedayita- ° 183:–*See also Cessation, of perception & feeling*
Nīvaraṇa 67, 109:–*See also Hindrances, five*
Noble truths, four (ariya-saccā) 5-11, 119, 130, 142, 143-145, 149, 182
Non-self (anattā) 14, 86, 87, 121, 122, 124, 130, 146, 155, 157, 161, 166, 167, 170, 173
Nothingness, sphere of (ākiñcaññāyatana) 27, 65, 105, 109, 110, 120, 183

O

Once-return, path of (sakadāgāmi-magga) 129, 143, 176, 179, 181
One-pointedness of mind (citt'ekaggatā) 41, 63, 142, 147
Overcoming (pahāna) 9, 88, 121, 122, 123, 182

P

Paccavekkhaṇa 181:–*See also Reviewing*
Paccaya-sannissita-sīla 57:–*See also Sīla, -visuddhi*
Pahāna 182:–*See also Overcoming*
Pain (dukkha) 6, 7, 9, 10, 16, 18, 23, 26, 34, 42, 78, 81, 98, 100, 116, 120, 131, 138, 140, 147, 150, 155, 163, 164
Pañcakhandha 5, 6, 64, 129, 130, 131-133, 143, 146:–*See also Groups of existence, five*
Paññā 5, 42, 129:–*See also Wisdom*
  ° -bhāvanā 64, 129
  ° -vimutta 174
  as a faculty 138, 142
  as one of ten perfections 105
  three kinds of ° 129
  vipassanā- ° 129
Paramattha 33, 118:–*See also Ultimate truth*
Pāramī, pāramitā 105:–*See also Perfections, ten*
Pariññā 182:–*See also Comprehension, full*
Pārisuddhi-sīla:–*See Sīla, -visuddhi*
Passaddhi 40, 90:–*See also Tranquility, as enlightenment factor*
Path (magga) 5, 8, 10, 33, 34, 40, 43, 75, 116, 119, 120, 142, 149, 152, 162, 163, 164, 167, 178, 182
  ° -consciousness (magga-citta) 130, 180, 181
  ° -knowledge (magga-ñāṇa) 182
  ° of stream-entry (sotāpatti-magga) 88, 129, 143, 179
  ° of once-return (sakadāgāmi-magga) 129, 143, 179
  ° of never-return (anāgāmi-magga) 129, 180
  ° of arahatship (arahatta-magga) 125, 129, 143, 176, 177, 180
  in the four noble truths 144-146
  middle ° 33
  noble eightfold ° (ariya-aṭṭhaṅgika-magga) 6, 7, 73
  supramundane ° (lokuttara) 147-148, 173
  threefold division of ° 41-43
Paṭicca-samuppāda 6, 130, 149:–*See also Dependent origination*
Pātimokkha 57-58
  -saṃvara-sīla 57:–*See also Sīla, -visuddhi*
Paṭipadā:–*See Progress*
  fourfold 176
  ° -ñāṇadassana-visuddhi 44, 168:–*See also Purity, of the knowledge and vision of progress*
Paṭisaṅkhānupassanā 169:–*See also Reflective contemplation*
Paṭivedha 144:–*See also Penetration*
Peace, contemplation of 65, 71, 91
Penetration (paṭivedha) 34, 144, 149
Perception (saññā) 87, 88, 92, 93, 108, 110, 150, 153
  as one of the five groups of existence (saññākkhanda) 72, 99, 119, 121, 129-136, 146, 150, 160, 169, 172
  ° of light (āloka-saññā) 70
  ° of the loathsomeness of food (āhāra-paṭikūla- saññā) 65, 111-112
  cessation of ° 121, 183, 185:–*See*

also Cessation, of perception & feeling
° of forms (rūpa-saññā) 108, 120
reflex ° (paṭigha-saññā) 108, 120
° of diversity (nānatta-saññā) 108, 109, 120
Perfections, ten (pāramī) 105-106
Perfect One, the 33, 37, 73, 141, 175, 176
what becomes of ° after death? 30-34, 33
Pīti 9, 40, 68, 89, 90, 167:–*See also Rapture*
Postures, four 116
Powers, four roads to (iddhipāda) 159, 179
Progress (paṭipadā) 41, 73
four ways of ° 176-178
purity of the knowledge and vision of ° 44-47, 168
Purity (visuddhi) 116, 120
seven stages of ° (satta-visuddhi) 44-47
° of morality (sīla-visuddhi) 44, 57
° of mind (citta-visuddhi) 39, 44, 44-45, 46, 63, 64
° of understanding (diṭṭhi-visuddhi) 34, 44, 155, 168
° of escaping doubt (kaṅkhāvītaraṇa-visuddhi) 44, 160-161, 168
° of the knowledge and vision regarding path and not-path (maggāmagga-ñāṇa-dassana-visuddhi) 165, 168
° of the knowledge and vision of progress (paṭipadā-ñāṇa-dassana-visuddhi) 168
° of knowledge and vision (ñāṇadassana-visuddhi) 44, 179
threefold moral ° 37-39:–*See also Wholesome, ten courses of ° karma*
Puthujjana 180:–*See also Wordling*

R

Rāga:–*See Greed & Lust*
° -carita 70
arūpa- ° 181
kāma- ° 181
rūpa- ° 181
Rapture (pīti) 56-57, 75, 84, 89
as a defilement of insight 167
as a factor of jhāna 9, 67, 68, 87, 102, 183
as factor of enlightnement (pīti-sambojjhaṅga) 40, 90, 112, 119, 179
Realization 6, 45, 116, 120, 183
° of the cessation of suffering (sacchikiriya) 182
Rebirth-process (uppatti-bhava) 16, 23, 147, 150-151, 154, 165
Reflective contemplation (paṭisaṅkhānupassanā) 169, 172-174
Requisites
° for concentration (sammāppadhāna) 41:–*See also Effort, right, the four*
° of the monastitic life 57-59
Restraint 9, 51, 57, 86
Reviewing (paccavekkhaṇa) 181
Right understanding (sammā-diṭṭhi) 34, 37, 39, 41, 149, 159, 160-161
as part of noble eightfold path 8, 33, 147, 152, 163, 164, 179
conditions for its arising 36
mundane ° & supramundane ° (lokuttara-sammādiṭṭhi) 148-149
Roots, three (of kamma) 21
Round of rebirths (saṃsāra) 6, 22, 42, 92
immensity of ° 11-13, 99
Rūpakkhandha 131:–*See*

also Corporeality group

S

Sacchikiriya 182:-*See also Realization, of the cessation of suffering & Cessation, of suffering*
Saddhā 138, 141:-*See also Faith*
anusāri ° 174:-*See also Faith devotee*
vimutta ° 174:-*See also Faith, liberated by °*
Sadness (domanassa) 138-140
Sakadāgāmi 179, 181:-*See also Once-return, path of*
Samādhi 5, 9, 42, 63, 64, 129, 138, 142:-*See also Concentration*
sammā- ° 9, 63, 147
as part of bojjhaṅga 40, 90:-*See also Bojjhaṅga, seven*
parikamma- ° 63, 66
upacāra- ° 63, 67, 76, 109
appanā- ° 63, 67, 83, 109
Samatha 43, 64, 88, 159, 160:-*See also Tranquillity*
Sammā-ājīva 5, 8:-*See also Livelihood, right*
Sammāppadhāna 179:-*See also Effort, right, the four*
Sammā-vācā 5, 8:-*See also Speech, right*
Saṃsāra 6, 11, 12, 13:-*See also Round of rebirths*
Saṃyojana 180:-*See also Fetters, ten*
Sañcetanā 163:-*See also Voilition, manifested by body, speech or mind*
Saṅkhārā 23, 151, 153:-*See also Karma-formations*
Saṅkhār'upekkhā 169:-*See also Equanimity, regarding all formations*
Saññā 65, 70, 108, 109, 110, 111, 132, 150, 183:-*See also Perception*
ten, in Girimānanda sutta 121
Sati 5, 9, 40, 90, 115, 138, 142:-*See also Mindfulness*
Satipaṭṭhāna 81, 88, 159, 178:-*See also Mindfulness, the four applications of*
Satipaṭṭhāna Sutta 115-120
Selflessness (anattā) 64, 129
Sense bases (āyatana) 15, 23-24, 119, 122, 130, 135, 136, 138, 146, 147, 150, 154, 155, 165
Sex, as a moral precept 8, 17, 20, 38, 51, 52, 54
as gender 94, 131, 139
Signless deliverance (animitta-vimokkha) 173, 174
Sikkhā 42, 86:-*See also Training, threefold*
Sīla 5, 42, 43, 44, 51, 57:-*See also Morality*
° -visuddhi 57:-*See also Purity, of morality*
Sīla, samādhi, paññā 42:-*See also Path, threefold division of*
Similes:
ball of spittle 78
banana tree 172
blunt axe 72
bubble 78, 169, 172
butcher sits down at a junction 117
cart wheel rolling forward 81
cattle for slaughter 79
chariot 130, 155
cock's feather 77
dawn 34, 149
dewdrop 78
diamond 170
flood 81
furrow drawn in water 78
jugglery 172
lightning 168, 182
light of the moon 100
light of the stars 100
light or flame & wick 165, 182
lump of meat 78
mighty rock & silken cloth 12

mirage 172
mother protects child 100
mustard seed on pointed awl 168
oil-lamp 28, 64
phantom 169
piece of bowstring 77
rain 84
reed 172
ripened fruits 79
rocky mounts 80
sack filled with various grain 82
a saw 95
seed 22, 37
seven stagecoaches 44-47
solid rock & the wind 25
the sun rises 101
swivel-doll 158
untamed bull 72
wood-fire 92
wood and straw 158
Somanassa 138:–*See also Gladness*
Speech 133, 153, 159, 164, 183
common ° (vohāra-vacana) 118
inner- ° (vitakka-vicāra) 68
right ° (sammā-vācā) 5, 8, 33, 37-38, 43, 44, 51, 147-148, 152, 163, 179
vulgar ° 39
Spiritual powers (abhiññā) 106, 124
Subconsciousness (bhavaṅga) 136, 138, 165
Suffering (dukkha) 13, 14, 22, 31-32, 37, 86, 150, 167
cause of ° 16
cessation of ° 23, 26, 27, 28, 29, 154, 155
contemplation on ° 87, 119, 173
dependent origination of ° 15
noble truth of ° 5-8, 40, 43, 73, 142, 143-146, 149, 152, 182
Sukha 9, 68, 89, 138, 140
Supramundane (lokuttara) 41, 125, 130, 147, 178

T

Taṇhā 6, 7, 15, 23, 160:–*See also Craving*
Taints (āsava) 26, 43, 125, 151, 152, 161, 174-175, 177, 181
Terror, awareness of (bhayatupaṭṭhāna) 169
Thought conception (vitakka) 68, 87, 102, 132, 137, 183, 184
Training, threefold (sikkhā) 42, 63, 86
Tranquillity (samatha) 9, 43, 56-57, 67, 88, 124, 159, 160, 167
as factor of enlightenment (passaddhi) 40, 90, 112, 119, 179
development of ° (samatha-bhāvanā) 64-65
Truth devotee (dhammānusāri) 174
Turning away, contemplation of (nibbidānupassanā) 56, 87, 169, 171, 172, 180

U

Ubhatobhāga-vimutta 174:–*See also Both-ways liberated*
Uccheda-vāda 7, 146:–*See also Annihilation view*
Udayabbayānupassanā 169:–*See also Arising and passing*
Ultimate truth (paramattha) 33, 81, 99, 118:–*See also Conventional language*
Unsatisfactoriness (dukkha) 64, 129
[karmically] Unwholesome (akusala) 9-10, 18, 35-36, 39-40, 43, 53, 58, 63, 77, 84-85, 88, 97, 102, 105, 122, 133-134, 137, 141, 141-143, 151, 153, 163, 179
Upādāna:–*See Clinging*
° -(k)khandha 6, 146:–*See also Attachment-Groups*
Upadhi:–*See Worldly things*
Upekkhā 10, 40, 65, 68, 91, 102, 106, 1

38, 140, 169:–*See also Equanimity & Indifference*
Uppatti-bhava 154:–*See also Rebirth-process*

V

Vāyāma, sammā 5, 9:–*See also Effort, right*
Vacī-:–*See Verbal function*
° viññatti 132
° sañcetanā 163:–*See also Volition, manifested in speech*
° saṅkhāra 68, 184:–*See also Thought conception & Discursive thinking*
Vedanā:–*See Feeling*
°-(k)khandha 132:–*See also Feeling, as one of five groups of existence*
as component of nāma 150
as link in Dependent Origination 15, 23
threefold division of ° 140
Verbal function (vacī-) 51, 68, 132, 184, 185
Vibhava-diṭṭhi 7:–*See also Annihilation view*
Vicāra 9, 68, 102, 137:–*See also Discursive thinking*
Vimokkha:–*See Deliverance*
aṭṭha- ° 120:–*See also Deliverance, eightfold*
animitta- ° 173:–*See also Signless deliverance*
appaṇihita- ° 173:–*See also Desireless deliverance*
suññata- ° 173:–*See also Void deliverance*
Vimutti 91, 160:–*See also Deliverance*
Viññāṇa 15, 23, 133, 151, 152, 153:–*See also Consciousness*
Viññāṇa-kkhandha 133:–*See also Consciousness group*
Viññāṇañcāyatana 109:–*See also Boundless consciousness*
Vipassanā 43, 64, 72, 88, 125, 129, 159, 160, 166, 167, 178, 181:–*See also Insight*
Virāga 88:–*See also Detachment*
Viriya 40, 90, 105, 138, 141:–*See also Energy*
Visuddhi:–*See Purity*
satta- ° 44-47:–*See also Purity, seven stages of*
sīla- ° 57:–*See also Purity, of morality*
citta- ° 44, 63:–*See also Purity, of mind*
diṭṭhi- ° 155:–*See also Purity, of understanding*
kaṅkhā-vitaraṇa- ° 160:–*See also Purity, of escaping doubt*
maggāmagga-ñāṇadassana- ° 165:–*See also Purity, of the knowledge and vision regarding path and not-path*
paṭipadā-ñāṇadassana- ° 168:–*See also Purity, of the knowledge and vision of progress*
ñāṇadassana- ° 179:–*See also Purity, of knowledge and vision*
Vitakka 9, 68, 70, 102, 137:–*See also Thought conception*
-carita 70:–*See also Mentally unsteady nature*
Vohāra-vacana 33, 118:–*See also Conventional language*
Void deliverance (suññata-vimokkha) 173
Volition (cetanā) 51, 53, 72, 110, 111, 132, 150, 153, 163, 164
manifested by body, speech or mind (sañcetanā) 163

W

[karmically] Wholesome (kusala) 9-10, 18, 20, 35-37, 53, 63, 97, 105, 133, 137, 141, 143, 151, 153, 163, 17

9:–*See also Consciousness, karmically wholesome/unwholesome*
reward of ° morality 55-56
ten courses of ° karma 37-39
Wisdom (paññā) 5, 29, 133, 138, 178
as one of the ten perfections (pāramī) 105
as part of threefold division of the Path 41, 42-45, 63
development of ° (paññā-bhāvanā) 64, 129-130
higher ° (adhipaññā-sikkhā) 86
liberated by ° (paññā-vimutta) 174, 181
threefold ° (tevijjā) 125
World-period (kappa) 12
Worldling (puthujjana) 37, 46, 161, 180
Worldly things (upadhi) 29, 100

ABOUT PARIYATTI

Pariyatti is dedicated to providing affordable access to authentic teachings of the Buddha about the Dhamma theory (*pariyatti*) and practice (*paṭipatti*) of Vipassana meditation. A 501(c)(3) nonprofit charitable organization since 2002, Pariyatti is sustained by contributions from individuals who appreciate and want to share the incalculable value of the Dhamma teachings. We invite you to visit www.pariyatti.org to learn about our programs, services, and ways to support publishing and other undertakings.

Pariyatti Publishing Imprints

Vipassana Research Publications (focus on Vipassana as taught by S.N. Goenka in the tradition of Sayagyi U Ba Khin)

BPS Pariyatti Editions (selected titles from the Buddhist Publication Society, copublished by Pariyatti)

MPA Pariyatti Editions (selected titles from the Myanmar Pitaka Association, copublished by Pariyatti)

Pariyatti Digital Editions (audio and video titles, including discourses)

Pariyatti Press (classic titles returned to print and inspirational writing by contemporary authors)

Pariyatti enriches the world by

- disseminating the words of the Buddha,
- providing sustenance for the seeker's journey,
- illuminating the meditator's path.

www.ingramcontent.com/pod-product-compliance
Lightning Source LLC
Chambersburg PA
CBHW060823050426
42453CB00008B/563
* 9 7 8 1 6 8 1 7 2 3 4 3 3 *